Religion in Society

ISSUES

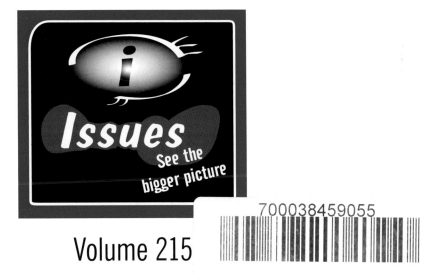

Volume 215

Series Editor

Lisa Firth

 *Independence*

Educational Publishers

Cambridge

First published by Independence

The Studio, High Green

Great Shelford

Cambridge CB22 5EG

England

© Independence 2011

British Library Cataloguing in Publication Data

Religion in society. -- (Issues ; v. 215)

1. Great Britain--Religion--21st century. 2. Great

Britain--Religious life and customs.

I. Series II. Firth, Lisa.

200.9'41-dc23

ISBN-13: 978 1 86168 595 7

Printed in Great Britain

MWL Print Group Ltd

CONTENTS

Chapter 1 Religion in the UK

Faith and culture in the community	1
What is humanism?	4
Religion and belief	5
Is religion a force for good in the world?	7
Religion today	8
Islam in the UK	9
Traditional practice may be down, but media coverage of religion is up	13
What is 'Christian Britain'?	14
Not atheist, not religious: typical Briton is a 'fuzzy believer'	15
Oxford study: belief in God is natural	16
Faith schools	17
Faith school admissions may promote social inequality	20
Does God belong in the classroom?	21

Chapter 2 Religious Tolerance

Religion or belief: rights at work	23
Has equalities legislation gone too far?	25
The law of England is not Christian	26
Islamophobia and anti-Muslim hate crime	28
Hatred of Muslims is one of the last bastions of British bigotry	31
British public most likely to blame the media for Islamophobia	33
Fear factor: Europe bans the burqa	34
Anti-Semitism worldwide, 2010	36
For and against the face veil	37
Two-thirds of Brits want burqa ban	39
Key Facts	40
Glossary	41
Index	42
Acknowledgements	43
Assignments	44

OTHER TITLES IN THE ISSUES SERIES

For more on these titles, visit: www.independence.co.uk

Sustainability and Environment ISBN 978 1 86168 419 6
A Classless Society? ISBN 978 1 86168 422 6
Migration and Population ISBN 978 1 86168 423 3
Sexual Orientation and Society ISBN 978 1 86168 440 0
The Gender Gap ISBN 978 1 86168 441 7
Domestic Abuse ISBN 978 1 86168 442 4
Travel and Tourism ISBN 978 1 86168 443 1
The Problem of Globalisation ISBN 978 1 86168 444 8
The Internet Revolution ISBN 978 1 86168 451 6
An Ageing Population ISBN 978 1 86168 452 3
Poverty and Exclusion ISBN 978 1 86168 453 0
Waste Issues ISBN 978 1 86168 454 7
Staying Fit ISBN 978 1 86168 455 4
Drugs in the UK ISBN 978 1 86168 456 1
The AIDS Crisis ISBN 978 1 86168 468 4
Bullying Issues ISBN 978 1 86168 469 1
Marriage and Cohabitation ISBN 978 1 86168 470 7
Our Human Rights ISBN 978 1 86168 471 4
Privacy and Surveillance ISBN 978 1 86168 472 1
The Animal Rights Debate ISBN 978 1 86168 473 8
Body Image and Self-Esteem ISBN 978 1 86168 484 4
Abortion – Rights and Ethics ISBN 978 1 86168 485 1
Racial and Ethnic Discrimination ISBN 978 1 86168 486 8
Sexual Health ISBN 978 1 86168 487 5
Selling Sex ISBN 978 1 86168 488 2
Citizenship and Participation ISBN 978 1 86168 489 9
Health Issues for Young People ISBN 978 1 86168 500 1
Crime in the UK ISBN 978 1 86168 501 8
Reproductive Ethics ISBN 978 1 86168 502 5
Tackling Child Abuse ISBN 978 1 86168 503 2
Money and Finances ISBN 978 1 86168 504 9
The Housing Issue ISBN 978 1 86168 505 6
Teenage Conceptions ISBN 978 1 86168 523 0
Work and Employment ISBN 978 1 86168 524 7
Understanding Eating Disorders ISBN 978 1 86168 525 4
Student Matters ISBN 978 1 86168 526 1
Cannabis Use ISBN 978 1 86168 527 8
Health and the State ISBN 978 1 86168 528 5
Tobacco and Health ISBN 978 1 86168 539 1
The Homeless Population ISBN 978 1 86168 540 7
Coping with Depression ISBN 978 1 86168 541 4
The Changing Family ISBN 978 1 86168 542 1
Bereavement and Grief ISBN 978 1 86168 543 8
Endangered Species ISBN 978 1 86168 544 5
Responsible Drinking ISBN 978 1 86168 555 1
Alternative Medicine ISBN 978 1 86168 560 5

Censorship Issues ISBN 978 1 86168 558 2
Living with Disability ISBN 978 1 86168 557 5
Sport and Society ISBN 978 1 86168 559 9
Self-Harming and Suicide ISBN 978 1 86168 556 8
Sustainable Transport ISBN 978 1 86168 572 8
Mental Wellbeing ISBN 978 1 86168 573 5
Child Exploitation ISBN 978 1 86168 574 2
The Gambling Problem ISBN 978 1 86168 575 9
The Energy Crisis ISBN 978 1 86168 576 6
Nutrition and Diet ISBN 978 1 86168 577 3
Coping with Stress ISBN 978 1 86168 582 7
Consumerism and Ethics ISBN 978 1 86168 583 4
Genetic Modification ISBN 978 1 86168 584 1
Education and Society ISBN 978 1 86168 585 8
The Media ISBN 978 1 86168 586 5
Biotechnology and Cloning ISBN 978 1 86168 587 2
International Terrorism ISBN 978 1 86168 592 6
The Armed Forces ISBN 978 1 86168 593 3
Vegetarian Diets ISBN 978 1 86168 594 0
Religion in Society ISBN 978 1 86168 595 7
Tackling Climate Change ISBN 978 1 86168 596 4
Euthanasia and Assisted Suicide ISBN 978 1 86168 597 1

A note on critical evaluation

Because the information reprinted here is from a number of different sources, readers should bear in mind the origin of the text and whether the source is likely to have a particular bias when presenting information (just as they would if undertaking their own research). It is hoped that, as you read about the many aspects of the issues explored in this book, you will critically evaluate the information presented. It is important that you decide whether you are being presented with facts or opinions. Does the writer give a biased or an unbiased report? If an opinion is being expressed, do you agree with the writer?

Religion in Society offers a useful starting point for those who need convenient access to information about the many issues involved. However, it is only a starting point. Following each article is a URL to the relevant organisation's website, which you may wish to visit for further information.

Faith and culture in the community

Information on the major faiths.

Buddhism

Buddhism began in Northern India over 2,500 years ago, and is based upon the teachings of Siddattha Gotoma who became known as the 'Buddha' – the enlightened one. After searching for a way to free himself and others from suffering, he discovered enlightenment. For the next 45 years he instructed those who were willing to listen in the methods to achieve this for themselves. Nothing was written down by the Buddha, but he left a legacy in the form of a teaching (the Dhamma) that was at first conveyed orally by the religious order the Sangha (a community of monks and nuns) that he founded and guided. Monks and nuns (mendicants) are not permitted to preach, they are spiritual companions who can only teach when asked to do so.

RIGHT THOUGHT · RIGHT ACTION
RIGHT MINDFULNESS · RIGHT SPEECH
RIGHT EFFORT · RIGHT UNDERSTANDING
RIGHT LIVELIHOOD · RIGHT CONCENTRATION

In order to help people realise that the normal understanding of life is inadequate, the Buddha spoke about 'dukkha' (roughly translated as unsatisfactoriness). He summarised his teachings as the Truth about 'dukkha'; its origin, its ending and the path to its ending. These core teachings were to be measured against one's experiences and used for guidance. They are known as the Four Noble Truths; first, that all life is unsatisfactory; second, that this springs from our craving. Complete happiness can be gained by the third, which is the absolute elimination of craving. This is achieved by the fourth Noble Truth, which comprises of following what is referred to as the The Noble Eightfold Path, i.e. the path of right understanding, right thought, right speech, right action, right livelihood, right effort, right mindfulness and right concentration. All eight components of this path are required to be developed together in order to achieve full enlightenment. The Dhammacakka Wheel represents the doctrine 'set rolling' by the Buddha: the eight-spoked Eightfold Path, the fourth Noble Truth and the Path to the end of suffering.

> ### Buddhism began in Northern India over 2,500 years ago, and is based upon the teachings of Siddattha Gotoma who became known as the 'Buddha'

Buddhism is divided into a number of different traditions and there are two main schools – The Theravada, or 'Teaching of the Elders', and Mahayana, or 'Greater Vehicle'.

Christianity

Christianity is based on the life, death and resurrection of Jesus Christ, who lived as a Jew in the Middle East. Christians date their calendar from his birth. The Christian holy book is the Bible, comprising the Jewish scriptures or Old Testament and the New Testament, about the life and teachings of Jesus Christ. Christians belong to the Church, which is a term used both to describe many of the buildings in which Christians meet, as well as the community of Christians who worship together, primarily on a Sunday. They pray regularly

WEST SUSSEX COUNTY COUNCIL

to the one God, whom they believe to have been revealed to the human race as Father, Son and Holy Spirit. The Cross is a symbol of the sacrificial death of Jesus, bringing forgiveness for human sins, and of his resurrection which opens the way to eternity. Belief and right behaviour are closely linked.

The Church is found in many forms: Orthodox, Roman Catholic, Anglican (e.g. Church of England) and many other types or traditions. Christians are people of all cultures and ethnicities and are numerically the largest of the world's religious groups.

Hinduism

The word 'Hinduism' is a collective term for the religious beliefs and practices of the Hindus. 'Hindu' was the word historically used of people living by the River Sindhu. The Hindu way of life is referred to as the Sanatana Dharma (the eternal religion) or Vedic Dharma (pertaining to the Vedas); it has no precise traceable beginning, nor is there a single founder. There is great diversity within the religion and its followers.

Hindus follow the sacred texts known as the Vedas (knowledge). They believe in an indescribable, all-encompassing oneness, an ultimate reality, referred to as Brahman.

> *The word 'Hinduism' is a collective term for the religious beliefs and practices of the Hindus. 'Hindu' was the word historically used of people living by the River Sindhu*

Brahman is depicted as having three aspects:

⇨ Brahma – the creator;

⇨ Vishnu – the sustainer;

⇨ Mahesh – the completer.

A central belief is in the existence of a cosmic or natural order, a balanced way of living, physically, socially, ethically and spiritually. These are interpreted as the four human achievements of:

⇨ Dharma – observing religious law;

⇨ Artha – acceptance of power, wealth and possession;

⇨ Kama – achieving quality and enjoyment of life in a balanced way;

⇨ Moksha – liberation from the continuous cycle of births and deaths (samsara).

Duty to others and taking responsibility for one's actions are fundamental to the notion of Dharma. Failure to do so results in a price to pay – Karma.

'Om' is the most sacred syllable often spoken during the practise of any Hindu rites. It is a holy character of the Sanskrit language, the language of God. The character is a composite of three different letters of the Sanskrit alphabet. The English equivalent of those are 'a', 'u' and 'm' and represent the Trimurti. The Trimurti is composed of the three supreme Hindu Gods: Brahma, the creator, Vishnu, the preserver and Shiva, the destroyer. These three letters when pronounced properly in unison create an invigorating effect in the body. Because of its significance this sacred syllable is spoken before any chants to show God we remember him. The sign in Hinduism also represents the whole universe.

Islam

The religion preached by the prophet Muhammad (SAW) 1,400 years ago is called Islam. Muhammad, God's messenger, taught that there is only one God (Allah). Believers in one God and Muhammad (SAW) as his messenger are called Muslims. There are different branches within Islam (as with Christianity). The two main ones are the Sunnis and Shi'ites.

The letters SAW are often seen after the Prophet's name:, this is as a mark of respect. They mean 'peace and blessings of Allah be upon him'.

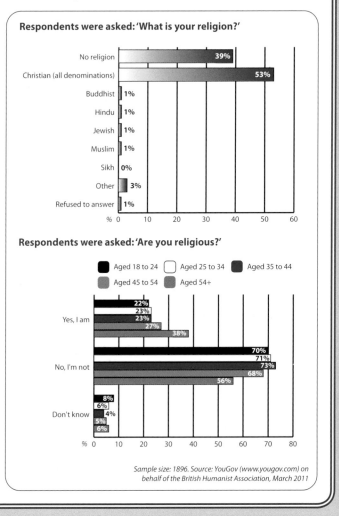

Respondents were asked: 'What is your religion?'

	%
No religion	39%
Christian (all denominations)	53%
Buddhist	1%
Hindu	1%
Jewish	1%
Muslim	1%
Sikh	0%
Other	3%
Refused to answer	1%

Respondents were asked: 'Are you religious?'

Aged 18 to 24 / Aged 25 to 34 / Aged 35 to 44 / Aged 45 to 54 / Aged 54+

Yes, I am	22% / 23% / 23% / 27% / 38%
No, I'm not	70% / 71% / 73% / 68% / 56%
Don't know	8% / 6% / 4% / 5% / 6%

Sample size: 1896. Source: YouGov (www.yougov.com) on behalf of the British Humanist Association, March 2011

The star and crescent moon is the centuries-old Islamic symbol.

Muslim belief entails submitting one's life to the will of Allah as revealed by the Prophet Muhammad (SAW) through the Qur'an and to do so through the declaration of faith, regular prayer, almsgiving (Zakat), fasting and pilgrimage. Muslims meet for prayers at a mosque. The main duties of a Muslim are summed up in the Five Pillars of Islam:

⇨ The Shahada – testimony of faith;

⇨ Salat – the obligation to pray five times a day: taking place at dawn (Fajar), midday (Zuhr), late afternoon (Asr), after sunset (Maghrib) and late evening (Isha), facing in the direction of the holy city of Mecca;

⇨ Zakat – to give a fixed 2.5% of one's income to charity;

⇨ Sawm – observe the fasting month of Ramadan;

⇨ Hajj – requires Muslims who are able to go on pilgrimage to Makkah (Mecca) once in their lifetime.

Muslims believe that God has sent many prophets throughout history to all the nations. All the prophets preached faith in one God, life after death and a moral code for life. The prophets include Abraham, Moses, Jesus and Muhammad (SAW). Muhammad (SAW) is considered to be the final prophet and the perfect model of how people are to live.

Prayers are obligatory from puberty onwards except for women who are menstruating or in the post-natal period. People who are not fully conscious are also exempted from prayers. Friday is the day for congregational prayers.

Judaism

Judaism is the faith of the Jews dating back over 4,000 years, originating in the Middle East. The Jewish community in Britain dates back to the Middle Ages.

The Jewish faith believes in one God, they do not believe in Jesus as the Son of God but believe there will be a Messiah in the future. The central belief in God is contained in the Shema, which is recited twice daily: 'Hear O Israel, the Lord our God, the Lord is One'. Jews believe that God has revealed his will for them, as revealed by Moses, in the Torah (The Holy Book), which is made up of the first five books of the Bible and sets out the Ten Commandments and the Talmud, a written collection of interpretations of the Bible and instructs on the Jewish way of life. The Jewish scriptures are known as the 'Tanakh' and worship can take place at a synagogue.

There are many Jewish traditions, which can be separated into two groups:

⇨ Orthodox – Orthodox Jewish people believe that the laws and teachings of the Torah must be followed today exactly as God passed them down in the time of Moses.

⇨ Non-Orthodox – non-Orthodox Jewish people, including those following Reformed or Progressive traditions, believe that some of the Torah's teachings can be adapted to be more relevant to a modern society.

Sikh

The Sikh tradition began in the Punjab region over 500 years ago. Sikhism was founded by Guru Nanak, the first Guru or teacher of the faith. There are about a half-million Sikhs living in the UK.

The word Sikh is derived from the Sanskrit word 'Sish', which means 'Disciple'. The Sikh religion is based on the teachings of Guru Nanak, supplemented by the successive Gurus, and is enshrined in the Guru Granth Sahib (the Sikh holy book). The tenth Guru, Guru Gobind Singh, stated that after him there will be no more human Gurus. Sikhs are ordered to accept Guru Granth Sahib (the Sikh scripture) as their Guru.

The Guru Granth Sahib is treated as a living Guru and is given the utmost respect. Sikhs meet for worship at the 'Gurdwara'. Gurdwara is a Punjabi word meaning 'gateway to the Guru'.

For Sikhs, there is only one God. God is without form or gender, everyone has direct access to God and everyone is equal before God. A good life is lived as part of a community, by living honestly and caring for others. Empty religious rituals and superstitions have no value. Sikhs believe in the equality of all human beings and respect all other faiths.

Many Sikhs expect to be initiated at some stage in their life. Belonging to the Khalsa involves taking amrit (nectar) and wearing the five articles of faith which distinguish individual men and women as members of the Khalsa, commonly known as 'the five Ks' because the Punjabi word for each begins with the sound of 'k'. The five Ks date from the creation of the Khalsa Panth by Guru Gobind Singh in 1699. Upon initiation, males take the name Singh (Lion) and females take the name Kaur (Princess).

⇨ The above information is an extract from the West Sussex County Council document *Faith & Culture in our Community*, and is reprinted with permission. Visit the West Sussex County Council website at www.westsussex.gov.uk for more information on this and related topics.

WEST SUSSEX COUNTY COUNCIL

What is humanism?

Information from the British Humanist Association.

Throughout recorded history there have been non-religious people who have believed that this life is the only life we have, that the universe is a natural phenomenon with no supernatural side, and that we can live ethical and fulfilling lives on the basis of reason and humanity.

Today, people who share these beliefs and values are called humanists and this combination of attitudes is called humanism. Many millions of people in Britain share this way of living and of looking at the world, but many of them have not heard the word 'humanist' and don't realise that it describes what they believe.

It is one of the main purposes of the British Humanist Association to increase public awareness of what humanism is, and to let the many millions of non-religious people in this country know that, far from being somehow deficient in their values, they have an outlook on life which is coherent and widely shared, which has inspired some of the world's greatest artists, writers, scientists, philosophers and social reformers, and which has a millennia-long tradition in both the Western and Eastern worlds.

[Humanism is] a non-religious philosophy, based on liberal human values

We also hope to give greater confidence to people whose beliefs are humanist by offering resources on our website and elsewhere that can develop their knowledge of humanist approaches to some of the big ethical, philosophical and existential questions in life.

Defining 'humanism'

Roughly speaking, the word 'humanist' has come to mean someone who:

⇨ trusts to the scientific method when it comes to understanding how the universe works and rejects the idea of the supernatural (and is therefore an atheist or agnostic);

⇨ makes their ethical decisions based on reason, empathy, and a concern for human beings and other sentient animals;

⇨ believes that, in the absence of an afterlife and any discernible purpose to the universe, human beings can act to give their own lives meaning by seeking happiness in this life and helping others to do the same.

However, definitions abound and there are longer and shorter versions. The fullest definition to have a measure of international agreement is contained in the 2002 Amsterdam Declaration of the International Humanist and Ethical Union. Some others include:

...a commitment to the perspective, interests and centrality of human persons; a belief in reason and autonomy as foundational aspects of human existence; a belief that reason, scepticism and the scientific method are the only appropriate instruments for discovering truth and structuring the human community; a belief that the foundations for ethics and society are to be found in autonomy and moral equality...

Concise Routledge Encyclopedia of Philosophy

An appeal to reason in contrast to revelation or religious authority as a means of finding out about the natural world and destiny of man, and also giving a grounding for morality... Humanist ethics is also distinguished by placing the end of moral action in the welfare of humanity rather than in fulfilling the will of God.

Oxford Companion to Philosophy

Believing that it is possible to live confidently without metaphysical or religious certainty and that all opinions are open to revision and correction, [humanists] see human flourishing as dependent on open communication, discussion, criticism and unforced consensus.

Cambridge Dictionary of Philosophy

That man should show respect to man, irrespective of class, race or creed, is fundamental to the humanist attitude to life. Among the fundamental moral principles, he would count those of freedom, justice, tolerance and happiness... the attitude that people can live an honest, meaningful life without following a formal religious creed.

Pears Cyclopaedia, 87th edition, 1978

Rejection of religion in favour of the advancement of humanity by its own efforts.

Collins Concise Dictionary

A non-religious philosophy, based on liberal human values.

Little Oxford Dictionary

⇨ The above information is reprinted with kind permission from the British Humanist Association. Visit www.humanism.org.uk for more information on this and other related topics.

© British Humanist Association 2011

Religion and belief

Some surveys and statistics.

Numerous surveys indicate that the proportion of individuals who do not hold religious beliefs is steadily increasing.

Religions and beliefs are notoriously difficult to measure, as they are not fixed or innate, and therefore any poll should be primarily treated as an indication of beliefs rather than a concrete measure.

However, one of the most well-respected measures of religious attitudes is the annual *British Social Attitudes* survey: further details of the latest report may be found on the NatCen website: www.natcen.ac.uk

Census data

The English and Welsh census uses the highly leading question 'What is your religion?'. By assuming that all participants held a religious belief, the question captured some kind of loose cultural affiliation, and as a result in 2001 over 70% of the population responded 'Christian'; a far higher percentage than nearly every other significant survey or poll on religious belief in the past decade.

The Office for National Statistics understands the religion question to be a proxy question for ethnicity. This is in order to capture the Jewish and Sikh populations, both of which are captured under race legislation but are not included in the ethnicity category in the census, as they should be, rather than the religion category. The result is that a very loose, cultural affiliation is 'measured' by the census in terms of religion or belief, with particular over-inflation of the Christian figure, and an undercounting of the non-religious population. As a result, the census data on religion is most definitely not suitable for use by employers or service providers.

2011 census polls

In a poll conducted by YouGov in March 2011 on behalf of the BHA, when asked the census question 'What is your religion?', 61% of people in England and Wales ticked a religious box (53.48% Christian and 7.22% other) while 39% ticked 'No religion'.

When the same sample was asked the follow-up question 'Are you religious?', only 29% of the same people said 'Yes' while 65% said 'No', meaning over half of those whom the census would count as having a religion said they were not religious.

Less than half (48%) of those who ticked 'Christian' said they believed that Jesus Christ was a real person who died and came back to life and was the son of God.

Asked when they had last attended a place of worship for religious reasons, most people in England and Wales (63%) had not attended in the past year, 43% of people last attended over a year ago and 20% of people had never attended. Only 9% of people had attended a place of worship within the last week.

The Humanist Society of Scotland commissioned a separate poll asking the Scottish Census question, 'What religion, religious denomination or body do you belong to?'. In response, 42% of the adult population in Scotland said 'None'.

When asked 'Are you religious?' 56% of the same sample said they were not and only 35% said they were.

The 2001 census

According to the 2001 UK census, those of no religion are the second largest belief group, about two and a half times as many as all the other (non-Christian) religions altogether – at 15.5% of the population. 7,274,290 people said they had 'no religion' – though only 10,357 specified that they were atheists. Jedi Knights had 390,127 followers, and formed a larger group than several of the 'major religions': Jews (259,927); Sikhs (329,358); Buddhists (144,453); or minor religions such as Jainism (15,132), Zoroastrianism (3,738) or the Baha'i faith (4,645).

Surveys and polls on religion and belief in the United Kingdom

In the UK, those who describe themselves as non-religious have risen from 31% to 51% between 1983 and 2009, according to the *British Social Attitudes* survey's 27th report issued in 2011.

An Ipsos MORI poll, published in January 2007 for the British Humanist Association, indicated that 36% of people – equivalent to around 17 million adults – are in fact humanist in their basic outlook.

Another question found that 41% endorsed the strong statement: 'This life is the only life we have and death is the end of our personal existence'. 62% chose 'Human nature by itself gives us an understanding of what is right and wrong', against 27% who said 'People need religious teachings in order to understand what is right and wrong'.

In a 2006 *Guardian*/ICM poll:

⇨ 63% of people say they are not religious (compared to 33% that are).

⇨ 82% of those questioned see religion as a cause of division and tension between people.

⇨ Only 17% of those polled believe the UK is best described as a Christian country.

BRITISH HUMANIST ASSOCIATION

In a MORI poll for the Catholic weekly *The Tablet*, published May 2005, the decline of religious belief is evident:

⇨ 36% of people in the 18-34 age group in Britain define themselves as atheist or agnostic.

⇨ In the population as a whole, 24% say they have no religion.

In the 2007-08 Citizenship Survey, participants were requested to select factors that they regarded as important to their identity from 13 options. Whilst family was top with 97%, followed by interests (87%), religion ranked bottom at 48%. Religion ranked bottom consistently with all age groups up to 65+, where it only moves up to 11th. Christians ranked religion as 13th as a factor important to their identity.

Church attendance in the UK

According to the 27th report (2010) of the *British Social Attitudes* survey, 20% of the population are affiliated with the Church of England (compared to 40% in 1983). The 26th report found that 49% of this group never attend services; only 8% of people who identify with the Church of England attend church weekly.

Overall, 62% of the population never attend any form of service.

According to *Religious Trends No 7 (2007-2008)*, published by Christian Research, overall church attendance in the United Kingdom has diminished rapidly, in terms of percentages and in real terms.

In 1990 5,595,600 people, representing 10% of the UK population, regularly attended Church; by 2005 this number had reduced to 3,926,300, equating to 6.7% of the UK population.

By 2015, the level of church attendance in the UK is predicted to fall to 3,081,500 people, or 5% of the population.

The Church of England's own attendance figures attest to the decline: between 2002 and 2008, average Sunday attendance figures have diminished from 1,005,000 to 960,000.

Religion and belief internationally

In September 2010, Ipsos conducted a 23-country poll on religion.

Of the 18,192 people who participated, 48% agreed 'religion provides the common values and ethical foundations that diverse societies need to thrive in the 21st century'.

However, 52% agreed with the statement 'religious beliefs promote intolerance, exacerbate ethnic divisions, and impede social progress in developing and developed nations alike'. With the exception of the United States of America, generally wealthy nations had a markedly more negative view of religion.

In 2007, Britain ranked 15th in the table that shows the top 50 countries with the largest percentage of people who identify themselves as either atheist, agnostic or a non-believer in God.

In 2004, the BBC commissioned an ICM poll in ten countries examining levels of belief. Participants from the United Kingdom tended to display markedly less religious belief than many of their counterparts. In response to the statement 'A belief in God (higher power) makes for a better human being', 43% of participants from the UK disagreed with this, substantially more than any other nationality.

In the United States the picture of belief is quite different: only 3% of people questioned in the American Religious Identification Survey stated they did not have a belief in God, and only 8% were doubtful. However, it is important to note that in the USA, as with most of Europe, there is a marked decline in the level of belief; in 1991, 86% of Americans identified as Christian: by 2008, this number had reduced to 72%.

Religion and Government

In the *British Social Attitudes* survey 2010:

⇨ 75% of those questioned believed their religious leaders should not influence their voting behaviour.

⇨ 67% believe religious leaders should stay out of Government decision-making.

⇨ 45% of Britons believe that the involvement of religious leaders would have a deleterious effect on policy.

⇨ Only 25% of people believe religious involvement would produce better policy.

⇨ 73% of respondents believe that 'people with very strong religious beliefs are often too intolerant of others'. This view was held by 82% of people who class themselves as non-religious, and 63% of those who consider themselves religious.

Bishops in the House of Lords

74% of the British public believe it is wrong that Bishops have an automatic right to a seat in the House of Lords, including 70% of Christians, according to an ICM survey conducted in 2010 on behalf of the Joseph Rowntree Reform Trust.

⇨ The above information is an extract from the British Humanist Association's article *Religion and belief*, and is reprinted with permission. Visit www.humanism.org.uk for more.

© British Humanist Association 2011

Is religion a force for good in the world?

Combined population of 23 major nations evenly divided in advance of Blair/Hitchens debate.

A new Ipsos poll commissioned for the 26 November Munk Debates on Religion in Toronto, Canada featuring Tony Blair and Christopher Hitchens has found that the world is evenly divided on one of history's most vexing questions: is religion a force for good in the world?

When the debate-framing question was put to 18,192 citizens of 23 nations worldwide, half (48%) agreed that 'religion provides the common values and ethical foundations that diverse societies need to thrive in the 21st century', whereas the other half (52%) agreed that 'deeply-held religious beliefs promote intolerance, exacerbate ethnic divisions, and impede social progress in developing and developed nations alike'.

On 26 November in Toronto, Canada, the Munk Debates is convening an international debate on the role of religion in the world. The debate will feature former British Prime Minister Tony Blair, a recent Catholic convert, debating author and atheist Christopher Hitchens on the resolution: 'Be it resolved, religion is a force for good in the world'.

Speaking about the debate, Mr Blair said: 'Understanding religion and people of faith is an essential part of understanding our increasingly globalised world.' Mr. Blair continued: 'The good that people of faith all over the world do every day, motivated by their religion, cannot be underestimated and should never be ignored.' Commenting on what it will be like to debate Mr. Blair, Christopher Hitchens remarked: '...he went "over to Rome" as soon as he could. Very bizarrely he did this at one of the most conservative times for the Catholic Church, under one of the most conservative Popes.'

The sold-out debate will be broadcast on the Internet live as a pay-per-view video feed at www.munkdebates. com starting at 7:00pm Eastern Standard Time. Edited versions of the debate will be broadcast on BBC World News (1 January 2011) and BBC World Service (date TBA). CBC radio in Canada and CPAC television in Canada will also broadcast the debate.

The key findings

The question put to respondents:

'In a world of globalisation and rapid social change some say religion provides the common values and ethical foundations that diverse societies need to thrive in the 21st century, while others say that deeply held religious beliefs promote intolerance, exacerbate ethnic divisions, and impede social progress in developing and developed nations alike... Which is closer to your own point of view?'

Those who believe religion provides the common values and ethical foundations that diverse societies need to thrive in the 21st century (48%) by country and region: Saudi Arabia 92%, Indonesia 91%, India 69%, Brazil 67%, South Africa 67%, United States 65%, South Korea 62%, Russia 59%, Mexico 51%, Italy 50%, Hungary 45%, Argentina 44%, Turkey 43%, Poland 42%, Canada 36%, Germany 36%, Australia 32%, Great Britain 29%, Japan 29%, Spain 25%, France 24%, Belgium 21% and Sweden 19%; Middle East/Africa 67%, BRIC 65%, APAC 57%, LATAM 54%, North America 51%, G8 countries 41% and Europe 32%.

Those who believe religious beliefs promote intolerance, exacerbate ethnic divisions and impede social progress in developing and developed nations alike (52%) by country and region: Sweden 81%, Belgium 79%, France 76%, Spain 75%, Great Britain 71%, Japan 71%, Australia 68%, Canada 64%, Germany 64%, Poland 58%, Turkey 57%, Argentina 56%, Hungary 55%, Italy 50%, Mexico 49%, Russia 41%, South Korea 38%, United States 35%, Brazil 33%, South Africa 33%, India 31%, Indonesia 9% and Saudi Arabia 8%; Europe 68%, G8 countries 59%, North America 49%, LATAM 46%, APAC 43%, BRIC 35% and Middle East/Africa 33%.

Some observations

⇨ Two countries with large Muslim populations had by far the highest percentage of respondents who agreed with the positive influence of religion: 92% in Saudi Arabia and 91% in Indonesia.

⇨ Countries with the lowest percentages in agreement with religion's positive impact were found in continental European countries such as Sweden (19%), Belgium (21%), France (24%) and Spain (25%).

⇨ Overall, developing economies had higher support for the positive impact of religion, with the Middle Eastern and BRIC countries averaging 67% and 65% respectively, and advanced economies of the G8 and Europe on the other end of the spectrum at 41% and 32%.

⇨ Of those who believe that religion has a negative impact, Western Europe stood out with large majorities in Sweden (81%), Belgium (79%), France (76%), Spain (75%) and Great Britain (71%) agreeing with the sharp statement that religious beliefs promote intolerance, exacerbate ethnic divisions

IPSOS GLOBAL @DVISORY

and impede social progress. On the opposite end of the spectrum were Indonesia and Saudi Arabia, with 9% and 8% support, respectively.

⇨ Citizens of Europe (68%) and the G8 (59%) were more likely to take this negative view than those from APAC (43%), BRIC (35%) or Middle Eastern and African countries (33%).

⇨ In North America there was a pronounced divide: in Canada only 36% agreed with the positive view of religion whereas 64% indicated it is a negative force in the world; in the United States it was the opposite: 65% in favour of religion's social role, and only 35% against.

⇨ In Turkey, a country divided between the European and Islamic worlds, the population was split, but leaned to a more negative than positive view of religion (57%-43%).

26 November 2010

⇨ The above information is reprinted with kind permission from Ipsos Global @dvisory. Visit www. ipsos-na.com for more information.

© *Ipsos Global @dvisory*

Religion today

***Findings from the 26th** British **Social Attitudes** report.*

Every year the *British Social Attitudes* survey asks around 3,000 people what it's like to live in Britain and how they think Britain is run. The survey tracks people's changing social, political and moral attitudes and informs the development of public policy.

Religion in Britain and the United States

There has been a sharp decline in religious faith in Britain, while in America people are much less likely to be atheist or agnostic. Despite this difference, people in Britain and America hold similar views about the place of religion in society. Most people are pragmatic: religion has personal and social benefits, but faith should not be taken too far. From politics to private life, many domains are seen as off limits to clerical involvement. Our research also revealed that just over half of people in Britain (52%) fear that the UK is deeply divided along religious lines and are particularly concerned about Islam compared with other faiths.

Just over half of people in Britain (52%) fear that the UK is deeply divided along religious lines

Religious faith and contemporary attitudes

People who are religious hold more traditional attitudes towards family and personal relationships. Half of religious people believe that homosexual sex is always or almost always wrong compared with one in five of non-religious people. One in five religious people agree that it is the man's job to earn money and the woman's job to stay at home and look after the home and family compared with one in ten of the non-religious.

April 2010

⇨ The above information is reprinted with kind permission from the National Centre for Social Research (NatCen). Visit www.natcen.ac.uk for more information.

© *NatCen*

Islam in the UK

Statements from the Islamic Society of Britain.

British Muslim identity and loyalty

Can you be British and Muslim? The answer is a resounding 'YES'.

Some years ago this was a debate within Muslim communities, particularly as first-generation migrants to this country felt culturally displaced from the countries of their origin. But for second- and third-generation people of Muslim heritage, Britain is their home. True, they may visit Pakistan, Bangladesh or other countries, but usually as holidaymakers, businessmen or to visit extended family, in the global village that we all now live in.

Increasingly, we have seen the presence of Islam in Britain take on a more 'British flavour' and this is something that the Islamic Society of Britain has been keen to nurture. Since its inception in 1990, the Society has been at the forefront of discussions to evolve a British Muslim identity. That journey may not be complete, but at least we can now see a community that is largely comfortable with its presence in our country and appreciative of the freedoms, progressive culture and democratic norms that British citizens enjoy.

Loyalty to the state is also an important aspect of this discussion. Muslims can be British, just as Jews, Christians, Hindus and people of other faith backgrounds. These identities are not at odds: rather, they operate at very different levels. Some Muslim scholars have gone as far as saying that when a point of tension exists between British interests and the interests of a Muslim nation abroad, then British citizens who are Muslims should support Britain by virtue of the social contract of citizenship they have entered into. At the end of the day, the yardstick will be justice – what is right – not based on 'who is my brother'.

Integration and cohesion

We are all citizens in a strong and proud nation, but one that can be more integrated. Citizens must show a willingness to get involved, interact with others and not isolate themselves.

The term 'integration' is often used in very different ways. To some it means people that have settled in this country should adapt and become 'more British' while having the freedom to preserve some of their inherited values and cultures; to others it means that one must leave one's cultural baggage at the door and dissolve into a melting pot of Britishness. The reality is that integration, acculturation or any such process of adaptation is never a simple process of one-way traffic.

Think of all the different people that have come to the UK over the last 60 years – people from the Caribbean, from Asia, Africa and more recently Eastern Europe – all have adapted themselves in some ways, but have also brought valuable things to these isles beyond the stereotypical corner shops and restaurants, exotic music and cinema, doctors' surgeries, taxis and cheap plumbing!

Muslim scholars agree that those who settle here should be loyal citizens to this country, and need to fit in – obvious examples are to learn the language and culture and to interact with other people. In fact, this can also be seen in the way that Muslims have adapted their practice of Islam to other regions of the world historically, such as India, Central Asia and parts of Africa and China. But we also need to remember that integration will involve a two-way process, of not whole communities being dissolved into a broader monolithic (and imagined) British culture, but becoming part of a changing British landscape that is diverse in itself.

Citizenship

A good Muslim should be a good citizen.

The term 'citizenship' is both a formal status – someone belonging to a state on the basis of a set of rights and duties – and, more importantly, a state of mind. Citizenship is not only about attaining rights, but more about participation in the political and civic process. To talk of citizenship, then, is to discuss rights, duties, participation and identity.

The Prophet Muhammad established a city-state in Madina and enacted a convention that laid down the basic rights and duties of its citizens. This form of 'social contract' in Islam is very similar to the idea of social contract that appeared in later European thought.

Some Muslims have debated whether one can vote in a non-Muslim society, or take up elected positions in a non-Islamic country. These are old debates, debunked time and again by credible Muslim scholars, and are irrelevant today, especially to Muslim citizens who feel a strong sense of belonging to their country.

Islam is not a religion of isolation and its basic purpose is to promote justice, peace and good relations between people. A good Muslim (indeed, a good human being) should be of service to all the people around them, as Muhammad taught:

'Whoever sees wrong, he should change it by his hands; if he could not do so, then he should change it by his tongue; if he could not do so, then he should do that by his heart, and that is the weakest of faith.'

Democracy

Most British Muslims cherish the democratic norms and traditions of Britain. While there may be a few people that reject democracy, this is an old debate that is now settled.

The acceptance of democracy was seen to be a controversial point some decades ago in certain Muslim circles. However, the point has been made that the Islamic sources do not identify a single model of governance; rather, values such as justice, accountability and equality of subjects do come across as prominent Islamic notions. Islamic practice sets precedence for strict accountability and transparency in leadership roles, where the head of state was described as the 'servant of the people' and the endorsement of the popular will was always paramount.

This was seen in the early history of Islam. But monarchy quickly became prevalent, under which dynastic rule became entrenched. The lawyers and scholars were at great pains to protect the domains of the courts and religious/civic institutions from the overbearing power of the state – leading to a *de facto* differentiation of powers and realms of authority, even if this was never historically articulated in the form of modern secular administration.

Many Muslim thinkers view democracy as a system that manifests the above values most authentically, however imperfect it may be. It is definitely preferable to monarchy, oligarchy or dictatorship, and in the words of Churchill, democracy could be seen as 'the worst form of government except all the others that have been tried'!

It must also be acknowledged that there is no single form of democracy; British, American, French, Canadian, Indian – all function differently with quite different constitutional frameworks, legal frameworks, relationships between religion and politics, etc. In this context, Muslim countries may also evolve new models of democracy, in which the rule of law, separation of powers, equality of citizens, freedom of speech and accountable governance can all be combined with respect for Islamic traditions and culture.

Violent extremism and terrorism

We have always had a clear and unequivocal stance against terrorism and those who advocate violence in our midst. Islam has never condoned the taking of life in this way. It is un-Islamic.

Terrorists at home or abroad, and their supporters in our midst, have a lot to answer for. They have taken the lives of innocents, they have spread mistrust and suspicion,

given implicit support to the voices of Islamophobes and bigots, not to mention the financial cost of their acts.

We support measures to tackle, prevent and stop terrorism, but are also critical of some of the initiatives and approaches that have been undertaken in this regard. Terrorism inspired by al-Qaeda can be best defeated in Britain by engaging and winning the support of local Muslim communities to help squeeze out the voices of violence and hatred. This requires using sensitively thought-out approaches, language and tactics and ensuring that the civil liberties of our nation are not trampled upon.

Suicide bombings

We do not condone the usage of suicide attacks in any context.

The tactic of 'suicide bombing' was adopted by some Muslim militants quite recently (1980s), taken up by Hezbollah and then others. Suicide bombing is heavily contested in Muslim circles. Very few scholars seem to have explicitly endorsed its usage as legitimate Islamic practice – e.g. some scholars have given limited license for its usage in conflict zones as a last course of action – however, this is not a consensus and particularly after 9/11 numerous scholars have been very critical of any form of suicide bombing. Among these one can count prominent Salafi scholars such as Shaykh ibn Uthaymin and Shaykh bin Baz before him, and Sufi scholars such as Shaykh bin Bayyah and Shaykh Afifi al-Akiti.

Commentators note that attacks involving a potential suicide dimension have been carried out throughout the ages by people from different religions and civilisations. Perhaps the oldest recorded story is of the Biblical Samson bringing the building down upon himself and his captors. Stories of the Knights Templar during the Crusades have also been recorded, and more recently the Kamikaze pilots of Japan reached notoriety.

A study by Robert Pape (University of Chicago) shows some interesting results. Pape has catalogued every act of suicide attack between 1980 and 2001. His results show that the largest number of attacks were conducted by the Tamil Tigers, a Marxist, atheist, revolutionary movement. This contradicts the popular assumption that suicide attacks are purely religiously motivated, and his study also shows that in every case a clear political objective lies behind the attacks.

Jihad

It is important to underline that 'Islam' means peace and aims for peace. As a last resort, and in exceptional circumstances, force may be used to defend oneself and others.

It is now more commonly understood that the word 'Jihad' means to struggle, to strive and to exert one's effort. As such it is a very broad term: one that has a very positive connotation and is a central doctrine in Islamic thought. Sometime the word is used to imply warfare – and this is simply because that would be seen as an extreme act of physical exertion. However, the Qur'an uses the term mostly in its broader meaning.

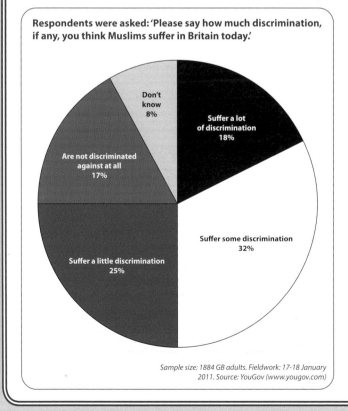

Respondents were asked: 'Please say how much discrimination, if any, you think Muslims suffer in Britain today.'

Don't know 8%

Suffer a lot of discrimination 18%

Are not discriminated against at all 17%

Suffer some discrimination 32%

Suffer a little discrimination 25%

Sample size: 1884 GB adults. Fieldwork: 17-18 January 2011. Source: YouGov (www.yougov.com)

Jihad is thus a part of everyday life for Muslims – waking up for the early morning prayer, controlling one's greed or anger, being kind to someone you do not like, working to better other people's lives, would all be seen as a part of the daily jihad. The Prophet said that the greatest act of jihad is to speak the truth in the face of a tyrant.

To extrapolate on the military context of the term (also known as the lesser jihad) – Islam does believe in a just war theory, like most Christian traditions, and envisages that violence can be used as a last resort in defence of one's life and property or to stem oppression: for example, if a country is invaded by an aggressor. Islamic traditions lay down very explicit conditions for the controlled and disciplined use of military aggression – even going as far as saying that animals, crops and trees should not be harmed, that innocent bystanders should not be attacked, that places of sanctuary such as churches and monasteries should not be desecrated and that as soon as the aggression stops the defensive force should also show restraint.

Sharia

We cherish the English Legal System and do not advocate the adoption of so-called 'Sharia laws' in the UK; we believe that the term is greatly misunderstood by Muslims and non-Muslims alike. The Sharia is really about justice and Britain is more just than most Muslim countries.

Sharia is an Arabic word that translates to 'the path' and describes a route to somewhere good. We mistakenly equate it with meaning 'Islamic law', but more accurately, the Sharia is a body of ethics and principles that should yield good laws. These ethics and principles come from the idea that by being fair towards his fellow humans, to animals and to the planet, man is serving God.

The Sharia wants to promote justice, protect people and stop harm – objectives which are to be found in most legal systems, particularly one that has evolved over time such as the English Common Law tradition. Where those objectives are met, the Sharia is present. In fact, the very early Muslims (including the Prophet Muhammad) didn't use the word 'Sharia' in its legal sense as we do today.

The word 'Sharia' provokes much unease and is also largely misunderstood – neither the Sharia nor the Qur'an contain express lists of fixed laws and rigid rules. Not surprisingly, a lot of this unease is related to the area of crime and punishment.

It is true that some of the punishments applied in some Muslim states are contrary to modern ideas of punishment. Ancient laws that predated the Qur'an by many centuries became part of the laws applied in the Muslim world during the early and medieval period of Islam. There are genuine questions to be asked (and are being asked) about the position of such punishments today, and some vigorous debates are taking place within areas of Islamic legal scholarship.

Gender equality

Men and women are equal in the sight of God, but sadly not in the sight of many people: this has to change.

There is much debate about this subject and it can't really be given justice in a few sentences. However, it is important to point out that in the name of Islam, there has been much misogynistic practice that has been carried out across the world.

Many would argue that this is due to regional cultural influences rather than the actual teachings of Islam as a faith, which seemed to have a remarkably emancipating approach for its time. One can see differential cultural influences at play in the Muslim world – so for example, in Malaysia one can find Muslim women who are business leaders, professors and highly educated academics, whereas in Saudi Arabia they are not allowed to drive cars, or in Afghanistan, even their basic education is contested by some!

Certainly the teachings of Muhammad tried to create a clear space for women in 7th century Arab society – they were recognised as individuals with their own agency, allowed to contract marriage, to own property, to engage in commercial transactions, allowed to inherit, to have a political voice, to become scholars and great teachers, etc. But some thinkers now acknowledge that cultural trends quickly changed and women were sidelined from the 'mainstream' and were left with quite distinct roles, mainly focusing on rearing and nurturing children. Perhaps this was the way of the world until very recently; after all, it was only in the 1970s that women in Switzerland got the vote, and only around World War II that women began to be seen commonly in the workplace in Europe. However, the advances made in Western nations, particularly in the latter half of the 20th century, have left many in the Muslim world quite dazed.

The current debate is therefore a crucial one, in which Muslim women (and men) – by re-examining the Islamic teachings in light of changes in the West – are beginning to articulate new positions and with an increasing confidence.

Polygamy

We are not in favour of the practice of polygamy for a number of reasons, not least of which, because it goes against both the letter and ethos of the law in this country.

There are different views amongst Muslim scholars on this subject. No doubt, there is a well-established body of Islamic thought that allows the marriage of a man to up to four women. But close scrutiny of this aspect of Muslim personal law and the teachings of the Qur'an show a very specific and limited context. The Qur'an says: 'If you fear that you shall not be able to deal justly with the orphans, marry women of your choice, two or three or four; but if you fear that you shall not be able to deal justly (with them), then only one...' (4:3).

According to some Muslim scholars, two important conditions are mentioned here – that the issue is raised in the context of a significant imbalance in population, in the context of warfare, in order to deal with the real situation of looking after orphans and widowed mothers, where a welfare state did not exist and single women were extremely vulnerable. The second condition is one of justice and equity between wives. A third important point is also that in the context of Arab culture at the time, the Qur'an was limiting the number of spouses (as previously men could marry an unlimited number of women), rather than encouraging this sort of marriage. This means that in ordinary situations, especially in a modern setting, the practice of polygamy is very difficult to defend.

Regardless of the theological and ethical debate, the bottom line is that this is not a positive requirement of Islam, it is an allowance, and thus if the law of this country has prohibited the practice this must be upheld.

Forced marriage

There is no place for forced marriage in Islam.

While the practice of forced marriage seems to be in decline, it does still raise its ugly head from time to time. Some have even tried to defend this cultural practice as 'Islamic'.

Islam is clear in giving the right to choose a partner to both the bride and the groom. Consent of both parties is an essential component of a valid marriage.

Forced marriages should not be confused with arranged marriages where, as is often the case in many cultures, extended families may suggest potential suitors, parents help in matchmaking, etc. This can be a perfectly acceptable tradition, so long as the couple are free to make their own choice of partner.

We adopt the Islamic view that a woman can propose marriage, give her own consent for marriage, can keep her family name, and if things go wrong, can also seek divorce of her own volition. She is not reliant on any male relatives for such matters.

⇨ The above information is reprinted with kind permission from the Islamic Society of Britain. Visit www.isb.org.uk for more information.

© Islamic Society of Britain

Traditional practice may be down, but media coverage of religion is up

Information from Religion & Society.

If you've felt that there's been increased discussion of religion in the British media in recent years, a new study shows that you're right. Coverage of popular religion, Christianity and public life, Islam and other religions and atheism and secularism has all gone up since the early 1980s. This is not restricted to news coverage, but is also evident in sports, entertainment and advertising; references to fate, angels, magic, ghosts, miracles and fortune telling are common. The single largest growth has been in coverage of Islam and it is overwhelmingly negative: Islam is presented as 'a problem'. But coverage of Christianity is also high. Why should this be, when over this same period church attendance and orthodox Christian belief have declined? It seems that the stock of Christian symbols and stories continues to provide a means for expressing wonder and fear, moral outrage and disgust, for praising celebrities and high achievers, contemplating the unexplained, and coping with unaccountable horror and crisis.

Professor Kim Knott led the research funded by the Religion & Society Programme that established these findings. She and her team conducted a replication of an investigation of media portrayals of religion first carried out in 1982-83. In 2008-09 she, Elisabeth Poole and Teemu Taira analysed a month's content from the same newspapers: *The Sun*, *The Times* and the *Yorkshire Evening Post*, and seven days' TV from the same channels: BBC 1, BBC 2 and ITV, using the same methods. In addition, they reflected the array of contemporary outputs by looking at *The Guardian*, the *Daily Mail*, Channel 4 and Sky News. They also ran focus groups with the public, and looked in detail at coverage of the banning of Dutch MP Geert Wilders in 2009 from entering the UK. An unexpected opportunity was also taken up to research media coverage of Pope Benedict's 2010 visit to the UK, as the first project had looked at Pope John Paul II's 1982 visit.

The team found that most references to Islam in the newspapers and on TV portray Muslims as extremists, terrorists and radicals. Other coverage, particularly in the tabloids, refers provocatively to the 'Islamification' of Britain, or shows Islam as problematic for social integration. The criminal and immoral behaviour of clergy often attracts media attention as well, and the liberal press frequently represent Christianity as anti-egalitarian and out-of-date on issues of gender and homosexuality. Newspapers and television attract audiences by focusing on conflict, deviance and, of course, celebrity. Freedom of speech, human rights, personal choice, and the belief that religion should be a private not public matter are just some of the secular – but nonetheless sacred – views discussed and often held by media professionals themselves. In sum, the growth of religious diversity has led to a rise in media references to all types of religion and belief. Religion is still reflected in the language of popular culture, and Christianity continues to be represented as part of national heritage and the British landscape. In a nation which is increasingly religiously-illiterate as a result of declining participation, the media are more important than ever for informing the public about religious matters.

3 May 2011

⇨ The above information is reprinted with kind permission from Religion & Society. Visit www.religionandsociety.org.uk for more information.

RELIGION & SOCIETY

What is 'Christian Britain'?

Information from Theos.

By Jonathan Chaplin

In their judgment in the Johns fostering case a couple of weeks ago, Justices Munby and Beatson declared that, although England has an established church, 'the laws and usages of the realm do not include Christianity, in whatever form'.

Whether or not the case ought ever to have been brought in the first place – the Evangelical Alliance questions this – the judgment is troubling at several levels. Whatever one's views of the appropriate criteria for fostering or whether the Johns met them, the case is a good deal more complex than some commentators have recognised. Although the judgment brings up a number of contentious points, perhaps the biggest question it raises is whether there is any longer a meaningful sense in which we can speak of Britain as 'Christian'.

There are (at least) four senses of the term 'Christian Britain'. The first is sociological. A nation could be termed 'Christian' if a significant majority of its population adheres to Christianity. If we take regular church attendance as an indicative benchmark, it's clear that only a minority – no more than ten per cent – of people resident in Britain is Christian. The figure is disputed and the forthcoming census is unlikely to resolve the argument, however people choose to respond to the British Humanist Association's appeal to the non-religious to come clean and state their true convictions. Justices Munby and Beatson are right to claim that Britain is clearly no longer Christian in this sociological sense, but rather 'a multi-cultural community of many faiths'.

The second is constitutional. There are two ways in which any state could qualify as constitutionally Christian: if its constitution explicitly endorses the Christian religion, as in article 44 of the 1937 Irish constitution, or if there is an established Church, as in England since (at least) 1534. England clearly is 'Christian' in this latter sense. 'Britain' is a more complex matter, yet in the words of the House of Lords Select Committee on Religious Offences in England and Wales: 'the constitution of the United Kingdom is rooted in faith – specifically the Christian faith exemplified by the established status of the Church of England... The United Kingdom is not a secular state.' In light of this, it is puzzling that the judges in the Johns case should declare that the laws of England 'do not include Christianity in whatever form'. Yet as an Anglican who has long favoured the progressive dismantling of the apparatus of establishment, this isn't a sense of Christian Britain I would man the ramparts for.

The third sense is historical. Prominent Christians are increasingly arguing that some of our fundamental political values – the rule of law, human rights, tolerance, democracy or hospitality to foreigners, for instance – were bequeathed in part by the historical legacy of Christianity (even if they were often resisted by some Christians) and that they will become threadbare if that legacy is repudiated by public institutions. This view is not limited to Christians; a version has been endorsed by the leading secularist philosopher Jürgen Habermas. I agree that something like it could be vindicated, but doing so would require a good deal of careful and inevitably contested historical argumentation. And even assuming such claims could be substantiated, it is not clear to me how they could resolve any contemporary political disagreements, vulnerable as they are to the flat response of Justices Munby and Beatson: 'that was then'.

There is, however, a fourth sense, which we might simply term 'democratic'. Suppose the great majority of the Christian minority in Britain acted publicly in ways consistent with the ethical implications of their Christian faith – in business, education, the environment, welfare, family life or foreign relations. Suppose they disavowed legal privilege and acknowledged their minority status alongside others in a plural democracy. Suppose they also allowed their principles consciously to shape their democratic activities as citizens, activists or office-holders, in ways appropriate to the specific remit of government. Suppose the cumulative influence of such Christian political engagement began over time to shape law, public policy, even judicial reasoning – challenging immoral arms trading, financial greed, unsustainable consumption, convenience abortion and easy divorce.

Gordon Brown seemed to be entertaining something like this in a thoughtful speech hosted by the Archbishop of Canterbury last month. Urging a rejection of both 'theocracy' and 'liberal secularism', he called for 'a strong faith politics which is part of an open and teeming public square, part of a deliberative politics that allows each citizen to bring the richest account of themselves to the public square'. The result would be a Britain in which effective and informed Christian democratic influence was brought to bear modestly, constructively and yet confidently – perhaps sometimes even decisively – on pressing issues of public justice. That's a 'Christian Britain' worth fighting for.

Jonathan Chaplin is Director of the Kirby Laing Institute for Christian Ethics and co-editor, with Nick Spencer, of God and Government.

14 March 2011

⇨ The above information is reprinted with kind permission from Theos. Visit www.theosthinktank.co.uk for more.

© Theos

THEOS

Not atheist, not religious: typical Briton is a 'fuzzy believer'

While secularism is on the increase, immigration from Poland and the Indian subcontinent could reverse this trend.

By Julian Glover

A blue plaque on a white stucco house just off the seafront in Brighton is a rare monument to atheism in a country where religion is a minority belief.

It marks the former home of George Holyoake, the last man to be jailed for refusing to believe in God and an overlooked hero of the secular cause.

Holyoake, a free-thinking radical, was jailed in Cheltenham in 1842 after suggesting, at the end of a lecture on socialism, that religion was a luxury the poor could not afford. The town's conservative establishment prosecuted him for his outspokenness – one priest called it devilism – and it is said he was threatened with being taken from Cheltenham to Gloucester jail in chains.

After his release from prison, he retreated for the last part of his life to Brighton. It was an appropriate refuge: the city is now, according to demographers, the least religious place in Britain.

Yet even today Holyoake would stand out as an exception in Brighton – a man prepared to speak confidently about his lack of belief rather than fudge the issue.

Most people in the Sussex city do not go to church: 27% said they had no religion in the last census. But most still described themselves as Christians. In Britain, cultural ties remain strong, even as belief fades.

'People here look at you a bit strangely if you say you are a regular churchgoer,' says Bill McIlroy, a member of Brighton's humanist and secular association. 'But while many people here don't believe, they have still got a misplaced respect for the church.'

That sense of tradition frustrates campaigners against the influence of what is now politely described as the faith community.

'People cling to the idea of religion as a source of morality,' says Terry Sanderson, president of the National Secular Society. 'There is a general apathy: people don't want to make a fuss.'

Many Britons have at best a shallow belief in God: the most recent *British Social Attitudes* survey found that just a third of the population held firm religious beliefs, with another third deeply sceptical and the final third uncertain.

But far fewer are prepared to go further and describe themselves as openly atheist. It was telling that Nick Clegg caused a stir when he did so soon after becoming Liberal Democrat leader.

'People prefer to talk about spirituality rather than religion, which can mean anything you want it to,' says Sanderson.

Even Holyoake – who went on to invent the term 'secularism' – professed himself more sceptical about religion than opposed. 'You cannot be an atheist – you do not look like one,' his memoirs record the magistrate telling him during his trial for blasphemy.

Holyoake held firm: 'Though sorry to say what might outrage them or look like obstinacy, yet out of respect to my own conscience I must say that I was an atheist.'

But by the end of his life he preferred to use the newly devised term 'agnostic'. That still best fits the mainstream British view.

According to demographer David Voas at Manchester University: 'The part of the population that is properly religious is a minority, but so is that part which is overtly secular. In the middle is an informal group of fuzzy people who don't really care.'

Britain is not, as some think, the most secular nation in Europe; it is less so than Scandinavia and parts of the former Soviet bloc.

Migrant communities are the most committed – even long-standing ones, such as Irish Catholics who dominate what Voas calls 'the British Bible Belt running from Merseyside to Wigan pier'.

Most other people are less engaged, although measuring belief is difficult and the data conflicting.

Much depends on how questions are asked and whether they refer to broad cultural identity or practical belief.

The census, which records the highest level of religious belief, assumes people are adherents of one religion or another and actively asks them to choose from a list.

In 2001, more than two-thirds selected 'Christian' and well under a fifth 'no religion'. That, says Voas, overstates the reality of British religious belief. Asked to choose 'Christian' rather than 'Muslim' or 'Hindu', people see it as an ethnic identity. Voas argues that

THE GUARDIAN

the *British Social Attitudes* survey, which found over half the population holding no strong religious views, is a better measure.

Other polls go further. In a 2006 *Guardian*/ICM poll only 33% described themselves as religious, against 63% who said they were not – including a majority who described themselves more broadly as culturally Christian.

Women and older people were more likely than average to believe in a god, but overall only 13% said they went to a place of worship at least once a week. More people saw religion as a force for harm than for good.

That suggests a country where religion is on the retreat. 'There is a huge change – the trend is towards secularism,' says Sanderson.

Others, pointing to the impact of migration, from Catholic Poland as well as the Indian subcontinent, are less sure.

The country's religious makeup is fragmenting as the Church of England declines. 'It is not the case that Britain is getting more religious,' says Voas.

The Pope will find himself on an island full of doubters.

10 September 2010

Oxford study: belief in God is natural

A study led by academics at Oxford University has concluded that believing in gods and an afterlife is part of human nature.

By Amy Shank

The £1.9 million study was conducted in 20 countries and looked at whether such beliefs are learned or a natural human inclination.

It found that people living in cities in developed countries were less likely to have religious beliefs than those living in rural areas, and that people with religious beliefs may be more willing to cooperate as a society.

The researchers suggested that attempts to suppress religious beliefs would ultimately fail because human thought 'seems to be rooted to religious concepts'.

They found that it was especially natural for children under the age of five to believe in 'superhuman properties'.

In one test, young children were asked whether their mother would know the contents of a closed box.

Are you there?

Maybe he just doesn't feel like talking?

While children at the age of three were likely to think their mother would always know the contents of the box, by the age of four they started to understand that their mothers were not all-knowing.

Dr Justin Barrett, from Oxford University's Centre for Anthropology and Mind, noted that the findings did not amount to proof of the existence of God.

'This project does not set out to prove God or gods exist,' he said.

'Just because we find it easier to think in a particular way does not mean that it is true in fact.'

The co-director of the project, Professor Roger Trigg from the University of Oxford, said the research showed that religion was 'not just something for a peculiar few to do on Sundays instead of playing golf'.

'We have gathered a body of evidence that suggests that religion is a common fact of human nature across different societies,' he said.

'This suggests that attempts to suppress religion are likely to be short-lived as human thought seems to be rooted to religious concepts, such as the existence of supernatural agents or gods, and the possibility of an afterlife or pre-life.'

Christianity remains the world's largest religion, with around two billion followers worldwide. Islam is second, with 1.2 billion followers, followed by Hinduism, Buddhism and Judaism.

14 May 2011

⇨ Information from Christian Today. Visit www.christiantoday.com for more.

Faith schools

In recent years there have been widely-reported exchanges of views surrounding the issue of faith schools, particularly those in the state sector. Frequently contentious, the debate has reflected the concerns of a broad range of individuals and groups, within and outside education.

Many of those concerns centre on the role of all schools to promote social cohesion against a backdrop of increasing government interest and investment in faith schools. Government policy perceives faith schools as a vehicle for delivering higher academic achievements, increased parental choice and coherent morality systems for pupils. As the evidence on whether current faith schools actually deliver these objectives is mixed, it is highly questionable that their expansion will do so, and the Association of Teachers and Lecturers (ATL) believes that the resulting imbalance of education provision is too costly to justify this flawed approach.

In a country portrayed statistically as progressively secular and yet diverse, the existence of denominational schools within the state sector is increasingly anomalous. ATL recognises that some faith schools offer excellent teaching and are well integrated into their local community. However, ATL believes that the fragmentation of education opportunities for pupils is not a good starting point for a society which is beginning to acknowledge the dangers of segregation, the importance of community cohesion and of shared understandings and values. ATL believes that we need schools that embrace the diversity of the individuals within our community, not a diversity of institutions dividing pupils and staff on religious grounds.

Government funding and faith schools

The present status of faith schools stems from the 1944 Education Act, which settled a long-standing dispute between Church and state over control of schools. In return for a degree of autonomy, church authorities were required to contribute financially to their schools. In the intervening years, the role of the churches has declined in a society that has become increasingly secular and also more multi-faith. Yet subsequent legislation has given increased powers and freedoms to religious organisations in relation to the running of state-maintained faith schools while reducing their financial commitment. Faith schools receive grants (of up to 90 per cent of the total cost) towards capital costs of the buildings and 100 per cent of running costs (including teachers' salaries) from the state. Yet voluntary-aided faith schools are allowed to impose faith restrictions on employment, admissions, curriculum content and on school worship.

ATL believes that faith schools should be more accountable if they continue to receive this level of state funding. State funding should be earned through evidence of socially just educational practices and a widening of service to the whole community. It is, after all, the community that pays such a large proportion of their costs.

Admissions, segregation and community

ATL is concerned with research findings that indicate higher levels of segregation in those local authorities (LAs) with the highest numbers of faith schools, particularly those with restrictive admissions or curriculum. We know that this concern is shared by many others, both outside of and within religious organisations and communities. A number of religious spokespeople have also decried the separation of children by faith affiliation, pointing out the risks of ignorance (of others who are perceived to be different) in terms of misunderstandings, parallel lives and potential for conflict. The Cantle Report (2001) stated that, 'contact with other cultures should be a clear requirement for, and development of, the concept of citizenship education from September 2002, and possibly a condition of funding'.

ATL wants this duty, to ensure that pupils have contact with other cultures, placed on all schools. This is particularly important in faith schools where the risks of segregation may be higher.

However, ATL does not advocate a faith-blind approach in schools, since this would not acknowledge the complexity of community or the individuality of pupils. It is vitally important that our public culture, in this case our schools, is faith-sensitive, and avoids the blockading of faith communities into embattled, inward-looking and defensive enclaves.

ATL calls for faith schools to implement measures, through their admissions, curriculum and employment practices, to ensure that they minimise the risk of segregation and to promote the goal of community cohesion.

ATL recognises that faith schools operate a variety of admissions policies, often determined by the schools' mission and levels of subscription. ATL acknowledges that there are many faith schools in areas of high social deprivation which do not have selective admissions policies; their mission is to serve their local community through education regardless of the faith make-up of that community.

ATL

However, other faith schools see their mission as the transmission of religious belief and culture from one generation to another, and have closed admission procedures with the majority of places allocated to those from their own faith community. Recently, some religious groups have shown their determination to maintain autonomy over admissions. In autumn 2006, these religious bodies overturned Government plans to oblige faith schools to reserve up to 25 per cent of school places for pupils with other or no faith, where there is local demand.

The question of admissions not only relates to equality of access, but also the perceived academic success of faith schools. Research has shown that higher performance levels of faith schools occur in those with selective admissions procedures and that these higher rates of achievement are due to autonomous governance and admissions arrangements and not due to religious character. This is significant when we consider that one of the key drivers of Government expansion of faith schools is the perception of their higher academic success.

Compared to national averages, pupils in faith and autonomous schools are much less likely to be entitled to free school meals and are more likely to have English as their first language.

ATL recognises that changing the legal status and existing autonomy of state-maintained faith schools would be difficult and complex, considering the history, political background, current sensitivities and levels of influence practised by some of the main religious affiliations. As such, our position has been developed from what is currently possible and realistic. An aspect of it centres on the, now Ofsted-inspected, duty for all schools to show evidence of promoting community cohesion.

ATL calls for the development of a framework of civic engagement in which faith and non-faith schools can work together for the common good and contribute to a community culture that transcends particular religious and cultural identities.

ATL proposes that criteria related to the promotion of community cohesion should be linked to the level of autonomy granted to schools, including faith schools, such as freedoms over the setting of admissions procedures and the curriculum taught within the school. Schools would meet this criteria through evidence of a range of activities; from specific projects to promote community dialogue and increased understanding, to activity across the taught curriculum promoting values of community engagement and tolerance.

Therefore, restrictive admissions could not be legally set by a school that does not show evidence of promoting community cohesion throughout its practices. All schools should be supported in this duty by the relevant bodies, including the Commission on Integration and Cohesion.

However, ATL recognises the difficulties for schools in finding the time to incorporate anything new within an already overcrowded curriculum, particularly one narrowed through excessive testing. Furthermore, we believe the current system of ranking school performance in league tables to be antithetical to the goal of inter-school collaboration.

ATL therefore calls for an urgent review of current school accountability practice, particularly school performance league tables and high-stakes national testing, in order that community cohesion and school collaboration is more than an aspiration.

Equalities

There are numerous equalities issues on both sides of the faith schools debate. It is clear, from an equality standpoint, that supporters (be they teachers, parents, politicians or the general public) of Church of England, Roman Catholic and Jewish schools cannot claim rights for them that they are then uncomfortable being accorded to other faith schools, such as Muslim, Sikh, Hindu or other faiths.

There is a dilemma for those concerned with education when trying to weigh the need for all faiths to be treated equally against the need for balance in school provision. ATL believes that this will require some innovative responses, with little place for 'position' politics or unwillingness to change.

The rights of groups are often talked about in the same light as the rights of individuals, yet the aggregation of individual rights is problematic as the rights of the group can conflict with the rights of the individual. After all, we are not merely defined by membership of one group; there are many other facets of identity. One can be defined by location, class, profession, race, sexuality, interests and so on.

ATL cautions against the homogenisation of groups through a faith identity that fails to recognise the diversity within.

As a union that supports teachers, support staff and school leaders, ATL is highly concerned by the equality of employment opportunities in faith schools. Current arrangements are restrictive, particularly within voluntary-aided schools, to protect the religious character of these schools. Indeed, late amendments to the Education and Inspections Act 2006 allow voluntary-aided faith schools to stipulate the religious belief of all employees, including support staff. In addition, this act permits voluntary-controlled faith schools, which are fully funded by the LA, to do the same for headship applicants. ATL strongly opposes this extension of staff appointment prescription in faith schools.

ATL believes the rights of faith schools to select candidates on the basis of their religion to be discriminatory and calls for an immediate halt to any extension of this privilege to new categories of staff.

It is not only our members and teacher colleagues who lose out as a result of these selection practices but also schools and pupils. We know that there is a particular recruitment problem in faith schools. For headteacher positions, not only must the pool of candidates be of the same religion as the faith school but they must also fit within certain parameters of personal behaviour; for example, practising Catholics can be ruled out if they have chosen to live with their partner before marriage, been divorced or are openly gay. This problem of recruitment in faith schools will only worsen should the faith school sector expand and increasingly, schools, staff, pupils and their parents will lose out.

Those strongly in favour of faith schools often cite the rights of religious parents, as taxpayers, to ensure that their child has state schooling within a school that promotes their faith. However, in areas where faith schools are over-subscribed, there is a real risk that non-religious parents, who are also taxpayers, do not have the same rights of access. Also, should the number of faith schools substantially increase, many parents may lose the right to ensure that their child goes to a community, non-faith school. Increased parental choice, whilst a mantra of the current Government, is not without cost; one parent's choice (and their ability to exercise it) has an impact on the choice of others.

Ultimately, with regards to the more popular schools, choice is exercised far more by the school than by the parents.

ATL believes that, in order to aid community cohesion rather than promote the rights of one section of the community, parental choice for a place in a faith school must be treated as an equality issue.

ATL believes that all schools should promote a culture of questioning, knowledge, respect, acceptance that others hold different beliefs, exploration and affirmation of values. ATL also believes that schools should be places where learners can develop their own identities and sense of place in the world. ATL shares the concern of Amartya Sen (Nobel Prize winner and author of *Identity and Violence*, 2006) that focusing, through schooling, on only one aspect of identity can miss out or suppress other aspects of identity, particularly those that do not fit in with the ethos of the religious group. A striking example of this is where a young person, brought up within a particular religion, discovers their homosexuality. They can then often find it difficult to reconcile these two aspects of their identity.

Therefore, ATL reiterates that all schools, including faith schools, should have admissions and recruitment practices which are inclusive and appreciate the diversity of the school and community population by promoting dialogue and understanding.

Curriculum, worship and inclusive practice within faith schools

ATL recognises that tenets of the faith system impose restrictions on not only what is taught within faith schools but on how it is taught. The national curriculum, despite its current overburdened and overtested state, has a significant role within faith schools through its prescription of the taught curriculum.

ATL therefore welcomes the integration of independent faith schools into the maintained sector. Even within the state-maintained sector, faith schools have a number of freedoms from national curriculum criteria which non-faith schools do not have. ATL believes that all national curriculum subjects, particularly RE, personal, social and health education and citizenship, should be subject to the same criteria, monitoring and inspection within faith schools as experienced in non-faith schools.

Under current arrangements, faith schools have the freedom to ignore the National Framework for Religious Education and are not subject to the same Ofsted inspection arrangements of the subject. ATL believes that all schools should be equally subject to the edicts of local Standing Advisory Councils on Religious Education or to the National Framework and that RE in faith schools should be subject to the same inspection regime, with a clear definition of the criteria, as imposed on non-faith-maintained schools.

ATL recognises that one of the strengths of faith schools is their recognition of the religious identities of their pupils. In some faith schools, where the school population is religiously diverse, this can extend to all pupils. ATL, as the education union, is concerned with those community schools that fail to recognise the importance of religious belief to some or all of their pupils. ATL has a similar concern for those faith schools whose practices belie a respect for all faiths and beliefs, both within their school population and within the wider community.

ATL advocates a curriculum and practice in both faith and non-faith schools that recognises the diversity of the school population in terms of background, values and beliefs, and encourages those pupils and their experiences to enrich all aspects of the curriculum within the school.

ATL recognises much of the good practice within faith schools; this needs to be shared and collaboration facilitated within the LAs.

ATL believes that all schools, including faith schools, need to have a responsibility towards the common good, the greater community, and to be expected to show evidence of actively supporting this goal. It is also crucial that LAs are the final arbiters of what constitutes the common good and its related activities in the context of their communities.

Conclusion

ATL's concern regarding faith schools is not merely in response to the current status quo but because of what we perceive as a growing imbalance in terms of education provision in this country and the implications for the future.

ATL knows, through the history of faith schools themselves, that it is difficult to predict both conditions around subsidy and the groups to which they will be extended in the future. ATL believes that limits need to be set over the extent to which state funding will continue to support the opening of new faith schools. This is a particular concern at a time when there are an increasing number of ways in which religious bodies and groups can have a disproportionate influence on schools.

Indeed, it is not only the types of faith school which are expanding but also the mission of those already in existence; the Archbishops' Council's report (2001) stated that church schools were on a mission to secure 'the long-term well-being of the Church of England' with the duty to 'nourish those of the faith; encourage those of other faiths; challenge those who have no faith'. Certainly, the proliferation of faith schools will challenge many; those of no faith and also those who wish to embrace a wider concept of education where educating the child is paramount above the growth of an institution.

The issue of faith schools will not be easily resolved, with some of the main players entrenching and strengthening their own positions. ATL is advocating a best-fit solution within the current context. We believe that the right kind of question at this time (to paraphrase the theologian Miroslav Volf) is not about how to achieve the final reconciliation but what resources we need to live in peace in its absence.

ATL believes:

⇨ that new criteria should be developed for all faith schools which contain core curriculum requirements;

⇨ that faith schools should have flexible and reviewable admissions criteria, which take account of school and local needs;

⇨ that the primary aim of faith schools (expressed through their mission statements and practices) should be to educate pupils as responsible and compassionate global citizens with the skills and knowledge to question and understand the world around them and to respect the beliefs, cultures and opinions of others. The promotion of the faith group should be secondary to this education and pupil-focused aim. ATL calls for these and the other measures outlined in this paper to be carried out by faith schools, religious groups and relevant state bodies within a structure of accountability and support. There should also be clear links between levels of funding, rights received and evidence of progress achieved towards community cohesion and the teaching of a broad education for all pupils.

Accessed July 2011: http://www.atl.org.uk/policy-and-campaigns/policies/Faith-schools.asp

⇨ Information from the Association of Teachers and Lecturers (ATL). Visit www.atl.org.uk for more.

© ATL

Faith school admissions may promote social inequality

Information from the Runnymede Trust.

Faith schools' admission rules have unfair 'white middle-class' criteria and discriminate against immigrant applicants, says head of the Office of the Schools Adjudicator (OSA), Ian Craig.

The partially selective schools are permitted to favour members of their faith, with many operating on a points system. Prospective pupils have an increased chance of being accepted if, for example, their parents are involved in church-based volunteering.

However, critics have in the past argued that parents with less free time to spare or those lacking in skill at manoeuvring the often complicated points-based systems to their advantage are likely to lose out.

Craig said: 'We have come across points that benefit white middle-class areas and don't benefit the immigrant children in the community,' as reported in the *Guardian* newspaper. He added that the issue predominantly concerns Christian schools as they significantly outnumber other faith schools.

The points system assumes that parents have time to volunteer, and that they follow specifically Western European Christian practices. In some Eastern European countries, children are not baptised until they are one year old.

When surveyed, 88 per cent of local authorities believed that faith schools in their area were compliant with school admissions laws, when in reality just 47 per cent were, according to the OSA.

In an authoritative and comprehensive report on faith schools and community cohesion, Runnymede's director Rob Berkeley states: 'By taking an exclusivist approach, these schools are forced into making judgments not just about the declared faith affiliation of the parents, but also interpretations of the depth of commitment to a particular faith.'

3 November 2010

⇨ The above information is reprinted with kind permission from the Runnymede Trust. Visit www. runnymedetrust.org for more information.

© Runnymede Trust

Does God belong in the classroom?

Faith schools applying for 'free' status are one of Michael Gove's biggest headaches. In part two of his series, Richard Garner wonders how these institutions square with the Government's plans for multiculturalism.

As many as 100 parents braved gale-force winds on a Sunday to find out more about the new primary school opening on their doorstep. It was a testament to the appeal of the new school – the first state-sponsored Hindu school to be proposed under Education Secretary Michael Gove's flagship 'free' school policy. The school only has places for 60 pupils a year and will open its reception class for the first time this September.

The school, the Krishna Avanti primary school in Leicester, is modelled on an existing Hindu school already opened in Harrow, north-west London. It, like other faith school proposals for 'free' schools, has its opponents, those that think the plethora of religious schools being opened under the Gove initiative will destroy community cohesion and increase segregation on racial and religious grounds among pupils.

Certainly, the aims of the new Leicester school are laudable in attempting to overcome that. Its mission statement insists it will select 50 per cent of its pupils on religious grounds, i.e. they are members of the Hindu faith, and 50 per cent from non-Hindu backgrounds. It is not a disciple of the 'free' school movement – choosing this route because it is 'the only game in town' when it comes to getting the go-ahead for new schools.

Other Hindu schools are in the pipeline – a secondary school covering the Harrow/Barnet area in London, which is designed to become the first state-funded Hindu secondary school, and other projects in Barnet and Redbridge, east London.

The programme is intended to overcome the situation whereby there are a million Hindus in the UK but only 30 Hindu primary school places a year for them. It intends to follow the national curriculum – its religious education lessons will be taken up 50 per cent by learning about the Hindu faith and 50 per cent about other world religions. There will be a Hindu flavour to the culture of the school. Vegetarianism will be the order of the day and there will be an emphasis on yoga and meditation, aimed at calming children in preparation for their learning.

'This is a British school,' Naina Parmar, headteacher of the Harrow school and project mentor to the new 'free' school, told parents at the open evening. 'It is very important from the start that we talk about world-class learning for our pupils.'

The trouble is, not every faith school is as open about its philosophy as Krishna Avanti. At Etz Chaim, a Jewish primary school in Mill Hill, north London, the project organiser, Adam Dawson, will not say anything about his school's plans. He says the project has felt the backlash from previous articles, that have led to project members being likened to 'child abusers' and being told to 'go back to where they came from'. As a result, it does not believe in communicating through the media.

It is one of four faith schools in the first tranche of nine 'free' schools approved by Gove – the others are the Leicester Hindu school and a Christian primary school in Camden, north London – where there is a pressing problem of a lack of primary school places, and a second Christian school, the Discovery New School – an Anglican primary school in Crawley, West Sussex.

The Department for Education, in a *résumé* of the Etz Chaim project, says it will be 'inspired by the beliefs of the Jewish faith with respect to ethics, morality and the importance of family, community and helping others'. It says: 'The Jewish studies and secular curriculum will be fully integrated, with the Jewish studies curriculum equipping and motivating pupils to engage with the Jewish way of life and with their Jewish heritage and

THE INDEPENDENT

culture.' It adds: 'Etz Chaim will be a modern, Orthodox Jewish, one form entry primary school.'

There was initially some disagreement between the project organisers and the DfE over the Government's insistence that 50 per cent of places should be offered to non-Jewish families, but that has now been overcome. The project is backed by the Chief Rabbi, Dr Jonathan Sachs.

Then there is the proposal to open the Everyday Champions Academy in Newark, near Nottingham, put forward by a Christian evangelist group which has creationism as the heart of its belief. It says it will not teach creationism through the science curriculum but that evolution will only be taught as another theory – in contradiction to the demands of the national curriculum (although the 'free' schools will have the authority to ignore the national curriculum).

This is without doubt the most testing issue for Gove as he sifts through the proposals for 'free' schools. Keith Porteous Wood, executive director of the National Secular Society, points out that – at the very least – such schools will have to be monitored very carefully once they have opened to ensure they are standing by any pledges they make. He says that it would be possible to teach evolution as a theory, but a 'raised eyebrow' from the teacher could denote the attitude they really take to it. He is convinced there will be many more applications from 'extreme religious groups', who would not be able to set up a state-funded school in any other way. 'I think it holds a very worrying message for community cohesion,' he says.

He also wonders how the spread of faith schools squares with Prime Minister David Cameron's recent pronouncement that the age of multiculturalism was dead and that all groups should embrace the British culture. He particularly blames it for fostering Islamic extremism. 'It is the biggest mis-match [in policy] that I can remember in my 15 years of doing this,' he says. 'The Government is saying we must be concerned about multiculturalism but somehow – as far as schools are concerned – they are untouchable.' He says he could accept that it was difficult after embracing Christian, Jewish and Muslim schools to refuse other mainstream religions the opportunity to run their own schools, but that what is emerging will lead to more of a divide among the young 'on racial, ethnic, religious and cultural grounds'.

Back to the Leicester school. Its organisers acknowledge that – despite their commitment to taking in 50 per cent of pupils from a non-religious background – it will be difficult to attract such applications in the first year. They believe, though, that if they succeed and gain a good reputation in the neighbourhood, that will follow.

It is true that all the parents at the open day appeared to come from a Hindu background. Sandhir Patel, who

is considering the school for his four-year-old son Kyan, though, said the emphasis on learning about all the faiths appealed to him.

One suspects, though, considering the Hindu school's commitment to trying to attract a diverse intake, it may be one of the easier applications for Gove to rule on. Others will be much harder.

Other religious free schools

Leicester's first state-funded Hindu primary school is just one of four applications from faith-based projects to be included in the first tranche of nine 'free' school bids to be given the green light by Education Secretary Michael Gove, ready for opening this September.

The others include a Christian primary school in Camden, north London, in a church hall in an area where there are not enough places for the current primary school roll; the Mill Hill Jewish School, to be run upon Jewish Orthodox lines, and a second Jewish primary school in Haringey, also in north London.

Still lying in his pending tray is the bid for an evangelical Christian secondary school in Newark, Nottinghamshire, which has vowed that the creed of creationism will be central to its ethos.

Critics say that the weakness in the current 'free' school policy is over the policing arrangements once the school is open. They argue that a school can make a commitment to having a diverse intake but that the proof of the pudding will be in the eating.

24 March 2011

© The Independent

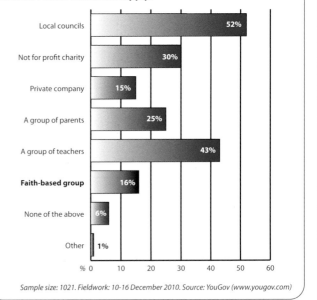

Respondents were asked: 'Suppose there was to be a new school built in your area that your child or children could attend. Which, if any, of these groups would be an appropriate group to run a school? Please tick all that apply.'

Group	%
Local councils	52%
Not for profit charity	30%
Private company	15%
A group of parents	25%
A group of teachers	43%
Faith-based group	16%
None of the above	6%
Other	1%

Sample size: 1021. Fieldwork: 10-16 December 2010. Source: YouGov (www.yougov.com)

THE INDEPENDENT

Religion or belief: rights at work

It is unlawful to discriminate against workers because of their religion or belief, or lack of religion or belief.

Employers should ensure they have policies in place which are designed to prevent discrimination in:

⇨ recruitment and selection;

⇨ determining pay;

⇨ training and development;

⇨ selection for promotion;

⇨ discipline and grievances;

⇨ countering bullying and harassment.

There is no specific list that sets out what religion or belief discrimination is. The law defines it as any religion, religious or philosophical belief. This includes all major religions, as well as less widely-practised ones.

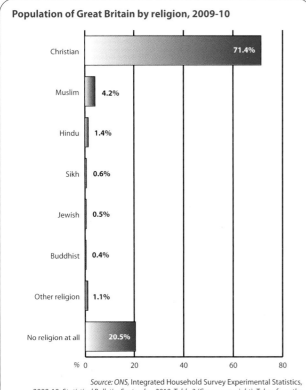

Population of Great Britain by religion, 2009-10

Religion	%
Christian	71.4%
Muslim	4.2%
Hindu	1.4%
Sikh	0.6%
Jewish	0.5%
Buddhist	0.4%
Other religion	1.1%
No religion at all	20.5%

Source: ONS, Integrated Household Survey Experimental Statistics, 2009-10, Statistical Bulletin, September 2010, Table 2 (Crown copyright). Taken from the EHRC document Religion or belief by David Perfect. The copyright and all other intellectual property rights in this material are owned by, or licensed to, the Commission for Equality and Human Rights, known as the Equality and Human Rights Commission ('the EHRC')

Employees are also protected against discrimination if they do not hold a particular (or any) religion or belief.

Your employer does not have to give you time off and facilities for religious observance but they should try to do so where possible

Many employers find that being sensitive to the cultural and religious needs of their employees makes good business sense. This can mean making provisions for:

⇨ flexible working;

⇨ religious holidays and time off to observe festivals and ceremonies;

⇨ prayer rooms with appropriate hygiene facilities;

⇨ dietary requirements in staff canteens and restaurants;

⇨ dress requirements.

Employee questions

Am I entitled to time off and facilities?

Your employer does not have to give you time off and facilities for religious observance but they should try to do so where possible. For example, if you need a prayer room and there is a suitable room available you should be allowed to use it, provided it does not disrupt others or your ability to do your job properly.

What can I do if I think I've been discriminated against?

If you feel you've been discriminated against, you'll be able to bring a claim to an Employment Tribunal. However, it's best to talk to your employer first to try to sort out the matter informally, in order to minimise the negative effects on all parties involved.

Through the Acas Helpline (08457 47 47 47) you can get advice on specific problems, and explore alternatives

ACAS

to an Employment Tribunal claim, such as mediation or Pre-Claim Conciliation, where appropriate.

Am I protected at work from discrimination against my religion or belief, or if I have no religion or belief?

Yes, the Equality Act 2010 protects workers from discrimination because of religion or belief as well as those who have no religion or belief.

The law means that an organisation's recruitment and selection procedures, as well as employment policies – such as dress codes and disciplinary procedures – must not unjustifiably discriminate because of religion or belief.

Am I allowed to wear clothing at work associated with my religion or belief?

If you wear clothing or jewellery for religious reasons, your employer should make sure that any dress code does not unjustifiably discriminate against you. In some circumstances, employers may have justifiable reasons for asking you not to wear particular clothing or jewellery; for example, health and safety or security requirements.

What does discrimination because of religion or belief cover?

Discrimination covers four areas:

⇨ Direct discrimination: treating someone less favourably because of their actual or perceived religion and belief, or because of the religion or belief of someone with whom they associate.

⇨ Indirect discrimination: can occur where there is a policy, practice or procedure which applies to all workers, but particularly disadvantages workers who hold a particular religion or belief.

Indirect discrimination can only be justified if it is a proportionate means of achieving a legitimate aim.

⇨ Harassment: when unwanted conduct related to religion or belief has the purpose or effect of violating an individual's dignity or creating an intimidating, hostile, degrading, humiliating or offensive environment for that individual.

⇨ Victimisation: unfair treatment of an employee who has made or supported a complaint about discrimination because of religion or belief.

What is the definition of a philosophical belief?

To be protected under the Equality Act, a philosophical belief must:

⇨ be genuinely held;

⇨ be a belief and not an opinion or viewpoint, based on the present state of information available;

⇨ be a belief as to a weighty and substantial aspect of human life and behaviour;

⇨ attain a certain level of cogency, seriousness, cohesion and importance;

⇨ be worthy of respect in a democratic society, compatible with human dignity and not conflict with the fundamental rights of others.

Humanism and atheism are examples of philosophical beliefs.

⇨ The above information is reprinted with kind permission from ACAS. Visit www.acas.org.uk for more information.

© ACAS

MY RELIGION HAS VARIOUS HOLIDAYS AND FESTIVALS...

SURE – WE DO HAVE CHRISTMAS AND EASTER OFF ...

Has equalities legislation gone too far?

Christian Concern equalities poll.

A ComRes survey published today suggests that the case of Owen and Eunice Johns (the Christian couple seeking to provide foster care in Derby) has prompted a significant shift in public opinion. The poll also highlights considerable public dissatisfaction with the current 'Equalities' framework and has prompted calls for urgent review and revision of the underlying legislation.

Following extensive media coverage of the case, only 30% of British adults now agree with the statement 'would-be foster carers who hold that homosexual activity is morally wrong should be banned from fostering', representing a fall of ten percentage points since the question was last asked, before the case hit the headlines following the high court judgment in March 2011.

Interestingly, the change in sentiment was most marked amongst those in the AB social grouping with support for the ban dropping by over a third, leaving only 23% in agreement.

The survey also revealed that the majority of the British public believe that 'Equalities legislation has gone too far', with 61% thinking that 'Britain has become a country where the right to exercise freedom of conscience is being trumped by equalities law'.

Given concern that the current Equalities framework is not fit for purpose, it is perhaps unsurprising that 84% agree that 'the Government should be required to review regularly the impact of equalities legislation on vulnerable groups and personal liberty'.

Following the experience of Owen and Eunice Johns and a string of similar cases, leading Christian advocacy group Christian Concern launched an 'Equalities and Conscience' petition, calling on the Prime Minister to ensure that 'the law provides a basis for widespread involvement in serving society whilst properly upholding the dignity of every individual, including those who seek to live with integrity to Christian conscience and teaching'.

Today's survey publication follows ComRes' November 2010 poll which had already highlighted widespread public support for freedom to manifest Christian faith and exercise Christian conscience without fear of penalty, and found that 72% of British adults agreed that 'Christians should be able to refuse to act against their conscience without being penalised by their employer' whilst 73% believed that 'the right of people to wear Christian symbols such as a cross in their workplaces should be protected by law'.

Commenting on the poll, Eunice Johns said:

'This survey suggests that when people see the end results of "Equalities" legislation their confidence in it drops. Ordinary people who seek to care for others are being unnecessarily excluded. Equality legislation seems to be ideologically driven. Our case has given the British public pause for thought and we hope that politicians will take note. These issues are not going to go away unless something is done. We need an urgent review of the existing law at the highest level.

'Our experience and a string of similar cases has revealed that the courts are unable to resolve these issues in an adequate manner, leading to the exclusion of those who seek the wellbeing of others. If the courts cannot address these matters, Parliament must. We urge all those who care about this situation, whether Christian or not, to support this petition for change.'

Andrea Minichiello Williams, CEO of Christian Concern, added:

'Cases such as that of Owen and Eunice Johns reveal what happens when legislation is framed with the aim of protecting and promoting an ideology rather than with actual people in mind. The current "Equalities" framework is unworkable and there is widespread public uncertainty about it. It fails to allow for the building of healthy, cohesive communities in which the dignity of every individual is upheld. We need rigorous debate and urgent review and revision.

'Christians want to participate in and serve our society, seeking the common good. Currently they make an enormous contribution but that is under threat. In fact, Christians will not be the only people affected by an increasingly oppressive and coercive regime that puts the pursuit of an ideological agenda ahead of the willingness of ordinary people to help others and to live according to their faith. We want to help Parliament to face up to and address this situation and create a better solution to these issues, for the good of all.'

ComRes interviewed 1,002 GB adults by telephone between 18 and 20 March 2011.

April 2011

⇨ The above information is reprinted with kind permission from ComRes and Christian Concern: visit www.comres.co.uk for more. The Christian Concern website also provides additional information on this and related issues: www.christianconcern.com

© *ComRes*

COMRES

The law of England is not Christian

The judgment in the case of a Pentecostal couple who wanted to foster children, but refused to accept homosexuality, is an important statement of secular principles.

The Christian Institute and similar bodies have mounted a series of court cases over the alleged persecution of Christians in the last five years. Almost all have been based around the claim that Christians are entitled to discriminate against gay people. Each one has ended in defeat. From the cross worn by Nadia Eweida to the attempts to allow religious exemption to the registrants of civil marriage, or the owners of B&Bs, the cases have been pitched as matters of high principle, and the judges have responded with increasing asperity. None, I think, has been so brutal as Lord Justice Munby in his judgment on the case of Owen and Eunice Johns, a couple of Sheffield Pentecostalists who were turned down as foster carers because they would not accept homosexuality.

'I cannot lie and I cannot hate, but I cannot tell a child that it is OK to be homosexual,' as Mrs Johns explained her position.

Now it is arguable that this is a case that could, and should, have been settled much more quietly. I believe that if you really 'can't lie and can't hate', or even if you have ordinary human difficulties with a policy of full-on lying and hating, then you must come to the view that for some people it is perfectly OK to be homosexual. But either way it isn't really an urgent problem. The Johnses were applying to foster children between the ages of five and ten, not teens troubled about their sexuality. It's absurd to make their views on homosexuality a shibboleth.

But the Johnses themselves, no doubt egged on by rich backers, decided to turn the case into a matter of principle. They wrote to the council: 'We take these statements and others to mean that it is either your policy, or your understanding of the law, that Christians and other faith groups who hold the view that any sexual union outside a marriage between a man and a woman is morally reprehensible are persons who are unfit to foster. In short you seem to be suggesting that Christians (such as us) can only adopt if we compromise our beliefs regarding sexual ethics.'

This is the view that Lord Justice Munby has described as a 'travesty of reality'. He goes on to say that:

'We are simply not here concerned with the grant or denial of State "benefits" to the claimants. No one is asserting that Christians (or, for that matter, Jews or Muslims) are not "fit and proper" persons to foster or adopt. No one is contending for a blanket ban. No one is seeking to de-legitimise Christianity or any other faith or belief. No one is seeking to force Christians or adherents of other faiths into the closet. No one is asserting that the claimants are bigots. No one is seeking to give Christians, Jews or Muslims or, indeed, peoples of any faith, a second-class status. On the contrary, it is fundamental to our law, to our polity and to our way of life, that everyone is equal: equal before the law and equal as a human being endowed with reason and entitled to dignity and respect.'

And it is the statements he goes on to make about 'what ought to be, but seemingly are not, well-understood principles regulating the relationship of religion and law in our society'. I am going to quote what follows at length, because it is a really clear statement of the status of establishment, and wholly in line with what has been said in other, similar recent cases where Paul Diamond made similar arguments:

'Although historically this country is part of the Christian West, and although it has an established Church which is Christian, there have been enormous changes in the social and religious life of our country over the last century. Our society is now pluralistic and largely secular. But one aspect of its pluralism is that we also now live in a multi-cultural community of many faiths. One of the paradoxes of our lives is that we live in a society which has at one and the same time become both increasingly secular but also increasingly diverse in religious affiliation.

'We sit as secular judges serving a multi-cultural community of many faiths. We are sworn (we quote the judicial oath) to "do right to all manner of people after the laws and usages of this realm, without fear or favour, affection or ill will". But the laws and usages of the realm do not include Christianity, in whatever form. The aphorism that "Christianity is part of the common law of England" is mere rhetoric; at least since the decision of the House of Lords in Bowman v Secular Society Limited [1917] AC 406 it has been impossible to contend that it is law...

'Religion – whatever the particular believer's faith – is no doubt something to be encouraged but it is not the business of government or of the secular courts, though the courts will, of course, pay every respect and give great weight to the individual's religious principles. Article 9 of the European Convention, after all, demands no less. The starting point of the common law is thus respect for an individual's religious principles coupled with an essentially neutral view of religious beliefs and benevolent tolerance of cultural and religious diversity.

'A secular judge must be wary of straying across the well-recognised divide between church and state. It is not for a judge to weigh one religion against another. The court recognises no religious distinctions and generally speaking passes no judgment on religious beliefs or on the tenets, doctrines or rules of any particular section of society. All are entitled to equal respect. And the civil courts are not concerned to adjudicate on purely religious issues, whether religious controversies within a religious community or between different religious communities.

'However, it is important to realise that reliance upon religious belief, however conscientious the belief and however ancient and respectable the religion, can never of itself immunise the believer from the reach of the secular law. And invocation of religious belief does not necessarily provide a defence to what is otherwise a valid claim.

'Some cultural beliefs and practices are simply treated by the law as being beyond the pale. Some manifestations of religious practice will be regulated if contrary to a child's welfare. One example is the belief that the infliction of corporal punishment is an integral part of the teaching and education of children and is efficacious... And some aspects of mainstream religious belief may even fall foul of public policy. A recent striking example is Westminster City Council v C and others [2008] EWCA Civ 198, [2009] Fam 11, where the Court of Appeal held on grounds of public policy that a "marriage" valid under both Sharia law and the *lex loci celebrationis* despite the manifest incapacity of one of the parties, was not entitled to recognition in English law.'

The judgment then went on to quote the (devout Anglican) Lord Justice Laws, when he rejected Mr Diamond's earlier case about an Islington registrar, another Pentecostalist, who wanted exemption on religious laws from performing civil partnerships. She had been supported by the former Archbishop of Canterbury, Lord Carey of Clifton. Laws was dismissive of their arguments, and said:

'The promulgation of law for the protection of a position held purely on religious grounds cannot therefore be justified; it is irrational, as preferring the subjective over the objective, but it is also divisive, capricious and arbitrary. We do not live in a society where all the people share uniform religious beliefs. The precepts of any one religion, any belief system, cannot, by force of their religious origins, sound any louder in the general law than the precepts of any other. If they did, those out in the cold would be less than citizens and our constitution would be on the way to a theocracy, which is of necessity autocratic. The law of a theocracy is dictated without option to the people, not made by their judges and governments. The individual conscience is free to accept such dictated law, but the state, if its people are to be free, has the burdensome duty of thinking for itself.

'So it is that the law must firmly safeguard the right to hold and express religious beliefs. Equally firmly, it must eschew any protection of such a belief's content in the name only of its religious credentials. Both principles are necessary conditions of a free and rational regime.'

Lord Munby added: 'We respectfully and emphatically agree with every word of that.'

Obviously, these judgments will have a considerable effect on evangelical Protestantism in this country, which has always taken the view that we are, or should be, a Christian nation. But I think the greatest effect will not be on Pentecostalists like the Johnses. They can adjust quite easily to the idea that they live under a heathen or godless regime. It is the old-fashioned evangelical wing of the Church of England which will be most upset and confused by these clear statements of principle.

28 February 2011

© Guardian News and Media Limited 2011

Islamophobia and anti-Muslim hate crime

Summary of research findings from Islamophobia and Anti-Muslim Hate Crime: UK case studies 2010. *An introduction to a ten-year Europe-wide research project.*

This summary divides our preliminary research findings into three categories: anti-Muslim hate crime; Islamophobia and discrimination; and responses and recommendations. We will produce full research findings in 2011 and beyond as we develop our research on this topic throughout the decade.

Anti-Muslim hate crime

The major part of our report introduces research findings in relation to intimidation and violence experienced by members of Muslim communities in the UK. It is based on over 12 months' close engagement with Muslim communities in the UK by a small team of researchers. In addition, some of the researchers have been engaged with the issue during the preceding decade.

The most significant findings derive from victims' first-hand accounts of violent crimes committed against mosques, Islamic centres and Muslim organisations; against Muslim women wearing hijabs, niqabs or burqas; and against Muslim men wearing distinctive Islamic clothes, in each instance offering compelling evidence of the existence of anti-Muslim hate crimes.

Muslims in the UK face a specific threat of violence and intimidation from politically-motivated attackers, and from gangs and individuals who are not aligned to extremist nationalism.

Terrorism and political violence against Muslims

Firstly, a small violent extremist nationalist *milieu* that has broadly the same political analysis as the British National Party (BNP), the English Defence League (EDL). EDL and BNP influence is significant but so is the influence of mainstream political commentators, which poses a threat of terrorism and political violence against Muslims. We therefore investigate a category of recent extremist nationalist criminal convictions that warrant the description of political violence (and often its sub-category, terrorism).

Hate crimes committed by gangs and individuals

The majority of anti-Muslim hate crimes in the UK do not appear to be committed by members or supporters of the EDL, BNP or their sister organisations and do not readily qualify as political violence for that reason. In London and other parts of the UK, gangs and individuals who have no allegiance with or affinity to the BNP, EDL

or the violent extremist nationalist *milieu* that surrounds those parties commit hate crimes against Muslims, Islamic institutions, Muslim organisations and mosques. Individuals who have become convinced and angry by negative portrayals of Muslims in the media, most especially of Muslims as terrorists and security threats, provide the main category of assailant.

Racist and random attacks

In addition, the vast majority of Muslims in the UK face additional threats of violence from violent racists and threats of random street violence that impact most severely on poor urban communities where most Muslims live.

Social impact of intimidation and violence

Intimidation and violence against Muslims are carried out by a minority of UK citizens to such an extent that it risks undermining and overshadowing the decent and responsible behaviour of the vast majority.

A burqa is a loose garment worn by women in some Islamic traditions for the purpose of hiding a female's body and face when out in public. It is worn over their usual daily clothing and removed when the woman returns to their household, out of the view of men that are not their immediate family members.

To what extent do you agree or disagree with the statement 'The burqa should be banned in Britain'?

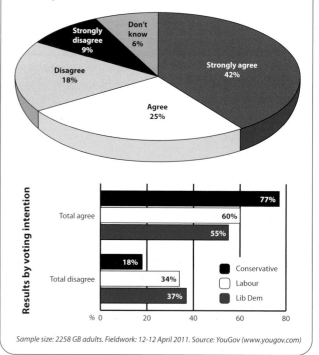

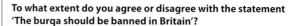

Sample size: 2258 GB adults. Fieldwork: 12-12 April 2011. Source: YouGov (www.yougov.com)

EUROPEAN MUSLIM RESEARCH CENTRE / UNIVERSITY OF ESSEX

Increased anti-Muslim intimidation and violence since 9/11

Since 9/11, Muslims in the UK have faced increased intimidation and violence because their faith or political activism has often been maliciously and falsely conflated with terrorism, extremism and subversion.

Plausible links between anti-Muslim hate crimes and media discourse

Assailants of Muslims are often motivated by a negative view of Muslims they have acquired from reports and commentaries in the media.

Many victims of anti-Muslim hate crime and Muslim victims of crime more generally do not report the incidents to police. Fear, suspicion and alienation are among a complex set of reasons for this situation

---

Hate crimes against mosques

Since 9/11, arson, criminal damage, violence and intimidation against mosques, Islamic institutions and Muslim organisations has increased dramatically. Many mosques in isolated Muslim communities have become particularly vulnerable.

Hate crimes against Muslim women

Our research reveals a disturbing number of hate crimes in which Muslim women wearing hijabs, niqabs or burqas have been assaulted, abused and intimidated. These incidents have taken place in public places – streets, shopping centres, on trains and on buses – invariably in view of passers-by and onlookers who have generally not intervened to help or defend the victims.

Muslim victims of street violence

On UK streets, violent attacks on Muslims are often demonstrably anti-Muslim in terms of motivation, while sometimes racist, sometimes anti-immigrant and occasionally purely random. In consequence, many Muslims face a greater cumulative threat of street violence than members of other minority communities and other fellow citizens.

Intimidation by the English Defence League

During the last two years there has been a dramatic rise in anti-Muslim demonstrations in Muslim communities by the EDL and sister organisations. These angry and often violent demonstrations increase fear and anxiety in Muslim communities.

Victims of 'Paki-bashing' are now victims of 'Muslim-bashing'

Many Asian and other minority ethnic Muslim families suffered racist violence and abuse in the UK in the 1970s, 1980s and 1990s and were cautiously optimistic that the problem was beginning to draw to a close at the dawn of the new millennium. After a brief respite that optimism has evaporated. Having endured National Front (NF)-inspired racist violence for decades they now face threats from BNP- and EDL-inspired anti-Muslim violence.

Serious under-reporting of anti-Muslim hate crimes

Many victims of anti-Muslim hate crime and Muslim victims of crime more generally do not report the incidents to police. Fear, suspicion and alienation are among a complex set of reasons for this situation.

EUROPEAN MUSLIM RESEARCH CENTRE / UNIVERSITY OF ESSEX

Insufficient data to establish scale of anti-Muslim hate crimes

Under-reporting by victims is one factor in a failure to establish the precise scale of the problem. Inadequate police procedures concerning anti-Muslim hate crimes is another important factor. An investigative focus on racist or anti-religious motivation often obscures a more straightforward anti-Muslim motivation.

Anti-Muslim hate crimes against isolated Muslim communities

Mosques and Muslims in relatively isolated and small Muslim communities are often at increased risk of anti-Muslim violence and abuse. Police support in some cases is inadequate to ensure the safety of mosques and worshippers.

Hate crimes against identifiable Muslims

Perpetrators of anti-Muslim hate crimes often show a sufficient level of awareness about the identities of their intended targets so as to carry out their attacks effectively. Hence attacks often take place in the vicinity of a mosque or against Muslims wearing Islamic clothes and, in the case of men, Islamic beards or, in the case of women, hijabs, niqabs or burqas.

Hate crimes against Muslim leaders and individuals

Muslim leaders who are wrongly demonised in sections of the media as 'extremist' or 'radical' face an increased risk of attack, abuse and hostility.

Islamophobia and discrimination

Our preliminary research findings deal with institutional Islamophobia as well as more general discrimination against Muslims. This tends to underline the findings of well-established if widely ignored research in the field. Our full report on the topic will be published in 2011.

Discrimination in politics

When dealing with discrimination against Muslims, Government ministers and parliamentarians are faced with a powerful lobby that argues forcefully against victim status for Muslims who face discrimination.

Discrimination against Muslim organisations

We find evidence of political discrimination against Muslim organisations. Both the previous Government and the new Coalition Government are influenced by negative advice from influential neo-conservative think tanks such as Policy Exchange, the Centre for Social Cohesion and Quilliam.

Discrimination by police and public servants

We have found evidence of institutional discrimination against mosques and Islamic centres in policing, local government and in local politics generally. This is not to overlook examples of good practice in policing, local government and local politics that have been recorded as well.

Recommendations

Anti-Muslim hate crime: urgent Government action needed

Violence and intimidation of Muslims and their places of worship and congregation has been at an unacceptable level since 9/11 and after a decade of neglect under the last New Labour administration, the new Coalition Government of Conservatives and Liberal Democrats has an opportunity to tackle it belatedly but before it becomes worse still.

Anti-Muslim hate crime: urgent community action and funding needed

The moral imperative of public safety is no less urgent for community activists, voluntary bodies and charities concerned to make an impact at the grass roots. Established campaigning groups will not need advice from us about the tactical advantage of pursuing genuine grassroots remedies and not simply of waiting for Government interest and support. Community projects like the Muslim Safety Forum (MSF) that aspire to support victims of anti-Muslim hate crime urgently need community funding and support.

Islamophobia and discrimination: political disinterest should be ended

We recommend Government and Parliament also begins to take the issue of Islamophobia and discrimination seriously after a decade of neglect. It is a litmus test for the new Coalition Government's commitment to fairness and social justice.

Political attacks against mainstream Muslim organisations should not be funded and supported by Government

Instead of funding divisive projects like Quilliam to denigrate and smear mainstream Muslim organisations, Government should adopt an inclusive approach to dialogue with Muslim community representatives. Urgent Government action is needed to help remove the stigma that attaches to many Muslim organisations at the forefront of tackling Islamophobia and other outstanding voluntary work in deprived communities in the UK.

⇨ The above information is an extract from the European Muslim Research Centre and University of Exeter's report *Islamophobia and Anti-Muslim Hate Crime: UK case studies 2010*, and is reprinted with permission. Visit www.exeter.ac.uk for more information.

© European Muslim Research Centre and University of Exeter 2011

EUROPEAN MUSLIM RESEARCH CENTRE / UNIVERSITY OF ESSEX

Hatred of Muslims is one of the last bastions of British bigotry

Baroness Warsi was right to speak out, says Peter Oborne.

It is not in the least surprising that Sayeeda Warsi's speech last night against Islamophobia has created anger. Many people will disagree profoundly with her claim that British Muslims suffer discrimination. This is because of the common assumption that Muslims have brought almost all of their problems on themselves, above all through their refusal to assimilate and play a full role in mainstream society.

Nor is that all. It is often claimed that Muslims have behaved differently from other immigrant groups, such as Sikhs or Hindus, by refusing to accept the legitimacy of the British state. Of course, there is some truth in this assertion. The Islamic political organisation Hizbut-Tahrir (to give one example) gives its fealty not to the national state but to the misty vision of an international caliphate, something which has not existed in substantive form since the collapse of the Ottoman empire in 1922.

The fear of terrorism adds greatly to the atmosphere of suspicion and there is no question that the London bombings in 2005, which killed 52 Britons and maimed many others, were linked in some perverted way to the religion of Islam. So I have no doubt that Norman Tebbit, one of my political heroes and a man of rare moral and physical courage, was speaking for many readers when he called on his *Telegraph* blog yesterday for a 'period of silence' from Baroness Warsi.

Yet I believe that the Baroness was right to make her speech and that Lord Tebbit was in the wrong. Indeed, I would go further and argue that the Baroness is showing exactly the same kind of moral courage that made Lord Tebbit such a towering figure among his time-serving colleagues in Margaret Thatcher's cabinets of the 1980s.

Baroness Warsi is not stupid. She would have calculated well in advance that yesterday's speech was a wretched career move. It is less than a week since she found herself in hot water after her injudicious remarks about the attitude of what she called the 'Tory Right' to the party's strategy in the Oldham East and Saddleworth by-election. The prudent reaction to this minor storm was to remain silent rather than grant fresh succour to her growing body of enemies inside the Conservative Party.

Instead, she has done the imprudent thing, and spoken out on an issue which is very close to her heart. In doing do, she has shown exactly the same kind of foolhardy moral courage for which Norman Tebbit became famous when he was Tory chairman, the post Baroness Warsi occupies today.

What she said yesterday has desperately needed saying by a mainstream politician for a very long time. I know this because, over the past few years, I have visited many Muslim communities and spoken to scores of Muslim leaders. With very few exceptions (such as Anjem Choudary, the fanatic who tried to organise a protest march by British Muslims through Wootton Bassett) they are decent people. Many have come from countries which persecute their citizens and trash human rights. So they are even more keenly aware of what it means to be a British citizen.

But – and this is why what Baroness Warsi has to say is so important – British Muslims get spat at, abused, insulted and physically attacked. Vandalism and mosque burnings are common, and often unrecorded. The far-right in Britain has changed its nature. In the 1980s, organisations such as the National Front and the BNP concentrated their hatred and odium on Blacks and Jews. Today, racist organisations such as the English Defence League focus on Muslim immigrants.

One of the most troubling things about this racist violence and abuse is that it is legitimised and made respectable by so much of the daily conversation which takes place in the media. Over the decades, Britain has learnt through ugly experience not to insult and discriminate against almost every other minority: Blacks, Jews, homosexuals, Irish. For some reason, Muslims are still seen as fair game.

Here is Martin Amis, arguably Britain's most famous living novelist, on the subject of Islam. 'There is a definite urge – don't you have it?' he told an interviewer, 'to say, "The Muslim community will have to suffer until it gets its house in order." What sort of suffering? Not letting them travel. Deportation – further down the road. Curtailing of freedoms. Strip-searching people who look like they're from the Middle East or from Pakistan.' In these remarks, Amis was doing rather more than insulting Muslims: he was using the language of fascism. And yet that did not prevent Amis's fellow author, the equally celebrated Ian McEwan, leaping to his defence.

Muslims are fair game in British public culture. Polly Toynbee of *The Guardian* is regarded as Britain's most politically-correct columnist. 'I am an Islamophobe and proud of it,' she once wrote. These sentiments were echoed by the rather less politically-correct polemicist Rod Liddle: 'Islamophobia: count me in'. Let's imagine for one moment that Toynbee had written instead: 'I am an anti-Semite and proud of it.' She would at once have been barred from mainstream journalism because anti-Semitism is rightly regarded as a noxious, evil creed. With Islam, by contrast, any insult is tolerated.

Many of our most famous newspapers – and not just the tabloids – routinely fabricate or pervert stories about Muslims. I have a bulging file of these malicious stories at home, and two of them concern Leicester University, where by coincidence Baroness Warsi was speaking yesterday.

One tabloid newspaper dramatically warned that thousands of hospital patients were in danger of catching superbugs because female Muslim medical students refused to follow new hygiene rules and bare their arms below the elbow. This was supposedly happening at Leicester University, so I went there to investigate for Channel 4's *Dispatches* programme, only to discover that not a single member of staff had come across any problems with hand-washing.

The students were shocked by the stories. One said: 'I always roll up my sleeves, and everyone that I know does.' The university told us that one student had asked a question about the new regulations, but had never objected to them. So there was a grain of truth, but it had been grossly distorted.

Above all, the insulting claim that Muslim medics were putting their religious beliefs before patients' safety was simply not backed up by evidence.

There is only space on this page to publish a tiny fraction of the evidence I have assembled which proves that hatred of Muslims is one of the last bastions of bigotry in Britain today. That is why I am so certain Baroness Warsi was right to speak out as she has.

It's important to stress that she wasn't demanding special treatment for Britain's two million-odd Muslims. She wasn't pretending they are all perfect, and she wasn't denying there is a big problem with terrorism which Muslims themselves must confront. All she was doing was making the very respectable and reasonable and urgent case that Muslims should be treated with the same courtesy as other Britons. Once he has read her speech carefully, I am sure that even Norman Tebbit, who is fundamentally such a decent and reasonable man, would agree.

20 January 2011

THE TELEGRAPH

British public most likely to blame the media for Islamophobia

Ahmadiyya Muslim Association UK Islamophobia survey from ComRes.

A new ComRes survey on Islamophobia – the fear of the Muslim faith – reveals that people think that the media is most to blame for whipping up a climate of fear of Islam in the UK.

People are twice as likely to say the media is to blame for Islamophobia (29%) than far-right groups (13%), or indeed Muslims themselves either abroad (14%) or in the UK (11%).

Conservative Party Chairman Sayeeda Warsi recently said Islamophobia had 'passed the dinner table test', becoming a social norm. Indeed, just 1% of people do not think that Islamophobia exists in the UK.

The poll was commissioned by one of the UK's oldest Muslim groups, the Ahmadiyya Muslim Community, in order to inform its plans to counter the tide of prejudice against Islam and highlight strategies to promote better community relations.

The poll comes on the eve of Britain's biggest annual Islamic convention which will see 30,000 members of the Ahmadiyya Muslim Community gathering at a 220-acre site in Hampshire. Foremost on the agenda will be ways to build bridges between communities and spread the word that Islam means peace.

Ahmadiyya Muslims recently launched a 'Muslims for Loyalty, Freedom & Peace' campaign with bus adverts, door-to-door pamphleting, fundraising for UK charities, blood donor sessions, inter-faith sessions, peace symposiums and more, across the UK.

Now, at the annual convention between 22-24 July, community members will reassert their ethos 'Love for All, Hatred for None' by pledging to counter hatemongers and extremism through a commitment to peace and amity.

Rafiq Hayat, National President of the Ahmadiyya Muslim Community, said:

'The results of the survey reveal that more needs to be done to refocus media attention on the valuable contributions Muslims make to Britain, rather than excessively focusing on the troublemakers who scream at us through media headlines but have nothing to do with Islam. Their nefarious activities do a disservice to this country and are an affront to our faith.

'The poll shows quite clearly that there needs to be greater positive engagement between the media and Muslims in order to address Islamophobia in the UK.'

Following the furore over the Pastor Jones controversy in the US, the ComRes survey also investigated perceptions over the Islamic scripture, the Holy Qur'an. Just 14% of the British public agree that the Qur'an justifies the use of violence against others.

'It is heartening to learn that the vast majority of people realise that there is no religious justification for terror and violence and the Holy Qur'an does not sanction hatred or discrimination. It states clearly that there is no compulsion in matters of religion.'

The survey does throw up other interesting results:

⇨ Muslims abroad (14%) are deemed to be more responsible than far-right political groups (13%) and UK Muslims (11%) for contributing to Islamophobia.

⇨ Younger people are more likely to think that the media is responsible for Islamophobia than older people – 40% of 18- to 24-year-olds think this, compared to just 18% of people 65 and over.

⇨ People who say that they do not belong to any religion (33%) are more likely to say that the media is responsible for Islamophobia than people who say that they are Christian (27%).

⇨ Just 7% of people from social group C1 agree that the Qur'an justifies the use of violence against non-Muslims – this compares to 17% of people from group AB, 16% from group C2 and 15% from group DE.

Andrew Hawkins, ComRes Chairman, said:

'Two-thirds of the public do not believe the Qur'an justifies the use of violence against non-Muslims, providing evidence of the public's predominantly tolerant, liberal view of religious minorities. British Muslims should also be encouraged that only one in ten of the British public believe they are to blame for Islamophobia. Instead, more than four in ten British people say the media or the far right are principally to blame for it.'

ComRes interviewed 1,004 GB adults by telephone between 8-10 July 2011. Data weighted to be demographically representative of all GB adults. ComRes is a member of the British Polling Council and abides by its rules.

July 2011

⇨ Information from ComRes: visit www.comres.co.uk for more. The following websites from the Ahmadiyya Muslim Community also provide further information: www.alislam.org, www.ahmadiyya.org.uk and www.loveforallhatredfornone.org

© *ComRes*

COMRES

Fear factor: Europe bans the burqa

Face-covering prohibitions in Europe are typically passed on the basis of three arguments: security, women's rights and secularism. Rational as they may seem, these arguments do not stand up to scrutiny.

By Herman Salton

About the author

Herman Salton is the author of *Veiled Threats? Islam, Headscarves and Religious Freedom in America and France*, 2008, 380pp. A researcher and freelance writer, he holds a degree in International Relations from Exeter College, Oxford University.

Fear has become the defining trait of contemporary Europe. A savage financial crisis, a single currency in disarray, Greece's economic turmoil and doubts about further EU integration are good reasons to worry about the future. Yet these are epiphenomena of more fundamental troubles, for Europe's systemic fears involve nothing less than the extent of her territorial and cultural boundaries. To put it bluntly, an aged Europe feels under threat from a world she once dominated, but which she never properly understood. It is this post-colonial world that is coming back to haunt her. And it is wearing a burqa.

A full veil with a grille through which women can see, this garment was originally introduced by the Taliban and quickly came to be seen in Europe as a sign of oppression, sexual discrimination and religious fundamentalism. Outside of Afghanistan, however, the burqa remains very unusual. Slightly more common, but still rare, is the niqab, where only a slit is left for the eyes. The headscarf, or hijab – a form of headgear that leaves the face uncovered – is by far the most widespread of Europe's 'foreign-looking' female apparels. In theory, these garments are subject to different legal treatments in Europe, with the hijab usually tolerated and face coverings increasingly restricted. As the French case suggests, however, in practice the difference is minimal – and shrinking.

Burqa = backward

Let us consider the 'burqa' first. In Europe, this word no longer refers to Afghan apparel, but has become a scary catchall for every form of female face-covering thought to be rooted in the Muslim religion (the parliamentary debates of several European countries are instructive on the point). This, however, is doubly incorrect, for neither the Afghan burqa, nor the niqab, are usually worn by Muslims. They stem from cultural rather than religious practices, and there is no trace of them in the Qur'an.

And yet, in a curious post-colonial turn, Islam has somehow become synonymous with face-coverings. There is no doubt that they are increasingly hated by Europe's politicians and their voters (who is influencing whom is hard to say). In Belgium, the Lower House passed a 'burqa' ban by 136 to 0 in April 2010, with usually-at-war Flemish and Walloon politicians rejoicing that the law restored 'a pride in being Belgian' (60% of the population support the ban). In France, President Sarkozy stated that the 'burqa' is 'a sign of submission which is unwelcome here' and, on 19 May 2010, vowed to outlaw it (57% of his fellow citizens agree, and the bill became law in September 2010). After making history for prohibiting the construction of new minarets – a move that was endorsed by 58% of the population – some of Switzerland's cantons are considering a 'burqa' ban, and so is the Dutch Government (with 66% support). In Spain, some city councils (such as

WE'RE PROTECTING YOUR RIGHTS!

UM, ISN'T THAT UP TO ME?

OPENDEMOCRACY

Barcelona) have banned the wearing of face coverings, while Zapatero's Education Minister supports a ban on Muslim headscarves at school. Although he eventually opposed a formal prohibition, Swedish Prime Minister Reinfeldt stated that 'we don't need to hide our faces in this way here' and indicated that he did not wish to see more women in 'burqas' (53% of Swedes would introduce a ban). Finally, in Denmark, a Government spokesperson made it clear that 'burqas and niqabs don't belong in Danish society', while in Italy, politicians are unearthing fascist-era legislation in order to fine the handful of women wearing face-coverings there.

A full veil with a grille through which women can see, [the burqa] was originally introduced by the Taliban and quickly came to be seen in Europe as a sign of oppression, sexual discrimination and religious fundamentalism

---

Such prohibitions are typically passed on the basis of three arguments: security, women's rights and secularism. After 9/11, security is an especially serious concern, and since face coverings hinder identification and have occasionally been used to commit crimes (such as bank robberies), banning them sounds reasonable to many. 'It is not about introducing any form of discrimination,' the Belgian MP who instigated the burqa ban bill said, 'it is aimed at forcing people to make themselves identifiable.' After all, several countries already have laws requiring visible faces in public, it is argued, so the ban has nothing to do with 'burqas' or indeed religion – as a Dutch Government spokesman put it, 'It's a safety measure: you don't see who's in it.' Women's rights are also routinely used to justify a prohibition of face veils: 'Burqas are contrary to the ideals we have of women's dignity,' Sarkozy stated, suggesting that they are demeaning regardless of the wearer's beliefs. Austria's women's minister agrees – 'I consider the burqa as a sign of the submission of women,' she declared – while a German minister defined it as 'a full-body prison'. Last but not least, face coverings are said to clash with Europe's hard-won division between Church and state. Having spent centuries fighting each other on religious grounds, most Europeans do not want to go back to a time when God, rather than the state, made decisions about public space. 'Other countries accept, without any problem or debate, visible religious signs in the public sphere,' one French MP stated, 'but it is not our case. We claim this choice; better still, we are proud of it.' Faced with fundamentalist Islam, a strong political signal was needed, a Dutch MP agreed, to 'give a political answer to a political problem'.

Rational as they may seem, these arguments do not stand up to scrutiny. Security is of course important, but face veils can hardly be regarded as a major threat. If there is a genuine belief that someone under a 'burqa' is a terrorist, police can invoke existing stop-and-search laws on grounds of reasonable suspicion, and Europe's few veiled women can be asked to lift them in certain situations (e.g. before entering a bank). There is, after all, a reason why the existing laws requiring clear faces in public remain mostly unapplied: not only are they invasive, they are also virtually impossible to enforce – and so much so that the proposed bans on face-coverings contain a plethora of curious exceptions (for funeral veils, carnival masks, motorcycle helmets, etc.). Moreover, numbers just do not support the view of the burqa as a security issue. In Belgium, this garment is worn by only about 30 women (out of a population of half a million, 3% of which is Muslim). In Switzerland, estimates mention 100 women covering their faces in total: 'If you have seen a burqa,' a local journalist commented, 'chances are the wearer was a rich tourist'. In Denmark, the centre-right Government abandoned plans to impose a ban after discovering that only three women in the entire country wear the burqa (around 200 wear niqabs). In Italy (population 56 million), there are only a few hundred face-covered women, while in France (population 60 million and home to Europe's largest Muslim minority), TV crews were at pains to find women wearing burqas (there are about 2,000 niqabs). Despite the stereotyped view of 'burqa'-covered terrorists, security threats involving this piece of clothing are rare and Europe's current witch-hunting climate makes it an unlikely catalyst for crime.

Women's rights are crucial and certain forms of veiling have historically been associated with misogyny (not only among Muslims but in most patriarchal societies). Sociological research, however, suggests that a growing number of women – especially young ones – do want to wear coverings for a variety of reasons: out of rebellion, as a statement of identity or modesty, for religious or traditional motives, and even as a fashion statement (the so-called 'Chanel veils'). Should we really be restricting women who choose to wear veils as a way of punishing those who force women to wear them? And will the day ever come when women can simply wear what they want, without any patronising intervention from overwhelmingly male legislators (or from their husbands)? It is of course encouraging to see so much interest in (and defence of) women's rights among Europe's male MPs. Centuries of barely-concealed misogyny, however, suggest some caution when assessing such passionate calls, not least because the most vocal supporters of the 'burqa' bans are often the most unlikely proponents of women's rights: not the left-leaning 'feminists', say, but right-wing parties (such as UKIP in the UK and the Northern League in Italy) that typically have little female representation except for the position of an equality spokesperson (one wonders why women should have a monopoly on this post, but I digress). So in Holland, for instance, hard-line immigration minister Rita Verdonk loudly invoked women's rights to oppose the burqa, but her ministerial record suggests that she was motivated by anti-Muslim prejudice more than anything else. The same can be said for Italian equality minister Mara Carfagna, whose personal story is instructive of how women's rights are easily trumpeted for political gains by unlikely defenders of female equality. A former show-girl, she is a junior member in the male-dominated Government of Silvio Berlusconi, a serial womaniser known for his sexist slurs who has openly admitted choosing his female aides on the basis of their physical appearance (he also dismissed Zapatero's government, which contained equal numbers of men and women, as 'too pink').

Last but not least, secularism is an especially rickety argument, for one only needs to look at the *de facto* dominance of public space that religion exercises in places like Poland and Italy, to see that Europe is hardly consistent when it comes to the separation of Church and state. Who can credibly argue that the ubiquitous presence of crucifixes in Italian classrooms is less of a threat to secularism than an individual's attire? Moreover, such contradictions are by no means confined to traditionally Catholic countries. In Germany, certain states (such as Bavaria and Baden-Württemberg) prohibit Muslim teachers from wearing the headscarf, but allow others to wear Christian clothing (such as the nun's habit). And even in supposedly hyper-secular France, strict *laïcité* is, like in most of Europe, *à la carte*: the majority of Catholic churches still belong to the French state and the French President is still *chanoine honoraire* (honorary clergyman) of the Lateran basilica in Rome (he is also the Prince of Andorra, a place where Catholicism is the official religion). More substantially, in some French regions Muslim girls are made to unveil before entering a classroom with a Christian crucifix. France happily allows exceptions to *laïcité* grounded on strong religious feelings in places like Alsace-Moselle for 2.5 million people (less than 5% of the population). But it does not cater for the needs of its five million-plus Muslim minority (10% of the same population).

8 November 2010

⇨ The above information is an extract from the openDemocracy article *Fear Factor: Europe bans the burqa*, and is reprinted with permission. Visit www.opendemocracy.net for more information.

© *openDemocracy*

Anti-Semitism worldwide, 2010

23% of all serious acts of violence and vandalism perpetrated against Jews and Jewish property globally in 2010 took place in the UK, according to Antisemitism Worldwide, 2010: General Analysis.

By Clive Field

This is a newly-published report from Tel Aviv University's Stephen Roth Institute for the Study of Contemporary Antisemitism and Racism and the Kantor Center for the Study of Contemporary European Jewry.

Of the worldwide total of 614 serious incidents in 2010, 144 were recorded in the UK, the highest number for any single country. France came next, with 134, and then Canada, on 99, followed a long way behind by Germany (38), the United States (28) and Australia (27).

The UK total was 61% down on that for 2009 (374 incidents), when anti-Semitism peaked in response to Israel's Operation Cast Lead in Gaza. This was larger than the 46% global decrease. UK anti-Semitism in 2010 was at a similar level to 2006 and 2007, according to the Tel Aviv data, but well above the double figures of previous years.

The publishers attribute the UK's pre-eminence in this global league table of anti-Semitism to the 'very unique' fact that Britain exhibits a strong presence of both far-right political groups and Muslim pro-Palestinian communities, each of which is viewed as being anti-Jewish.

It should be noted that the Tel Aviv researchers employ a far tighter definition of anti-Semitic incidents than does the Community Security Trust (CST), which has been monitoring anti-Semitism in the UK since 1984.

The UK [anti-Semitic incident] total was 61% down on that for 2009

The CST recorded 639 incidents in the UK in 2010 in its most recent report, which BRIN has covered at: http://www.brin.ac.uk/news/?p=855
May 2011

⇨ The above information is reprinted with kind permission from British Religion in Numbers (BRIN). Visit www.brin.ac.uk for more information.

© *University of Manchester*

OPENDEMOCRACY / UNIVERSITY OF MANCHESTER

For and against the face veil

Niqab-wearer and Muslim activist debate French move towards banning full Islamic veil.

By Indlieb Farazi

A French parliamentary panel has recommended that face-covering veils such as the burqa or the niqab be banned in public institutions such as hospitals and schools.

The decision is the result of a six-month inquiry into full veils, after Nicolas Sarkozy, the French President, said they were 'not welcome' in the country.

Here the issue is debated by Hadiah Ahmed, a niqab-wearing Muslim, and Shaaz Mahboob, vice-chair of British Muslims for Secular Democracy.

'The niqab is part of my identity'

Hadiah Ahmed, 30, is a full-time mother of two in Manchester. She previously worked as an interior designer in London. She says:

'I am a Muslim woman, born and bred in Yorkshire. I studied in English schools, furthered my education to degree level and have worked with celebrity faces.

'I changed my whole lifestyle for my religion as it was the way I wanted to live.

'I started wearing the khimaar (head scarf) and jilbab (a long dress-type cloak) a good few years ago as I started to practise Islam more, and it states in the Qur'an: "And say to the believing women that they should lower their gaze and guard their modesty." (24. 31).

'It was solely my decision, and after all, we live in Britain, a place where we have freedom of speech, freedom to live how we want to live!

'I can remember when I first went out in my hijab (Islamic dress), how people were staring at me and calling out things like "You bomber!"

'It was quite funny how, before I started wearing my hijab, men would whistle and make comments and now it was the total opposite. It's so strange how people perceive you just by what you wear even though you're the same person from within.

'I found that people were rude, talking to me as if I wasn't familiar with the English language and as if I was stupid.

'Sometimes it used to annoy me so much as I was educated in Britain, paid my taxes and yet I was being told to go back to my own country! Hello, I was born here!

'But now I just laugh and think that it's so ironic.

'Three years ago I went for pilgrimage to Mecca for Hajj and there it was when I decided to wear the niqab (a veil which leaves only the eyes uncovered).

'When I came back to England I kept on my niqab and the comments just escalated.

'Years on, I still get the looks and the comments. However, things are becoming increasingly harder for a Muslim woman wanting to practise her religion.

'In my opinion targeting the niqab is just an excuse to target Islam'

'In my opinion targeting the niqab is just an excuse to target Islam. After all, why is it that Christian nuns are not pinpointed for the way they dress?

'Or that it's OK to wear less and for women to be degraded and seen as sex symbols, but if someone wants to cover up and protect their modesty, then there's a big uproar?

'I, as a Muslim woman, should have the right to wear what I want without any question as to why I want to wear it. It's my identity, it's who I am.

'We are a hard-working family trying to practise our religion whilst living in a Western society.

'In my opinion governments should use their efforts wisely to try and promote unity so that religion and society can go hand in hand, so that we can live in peace.'

'The niqab has no place in Islam'

Shaaz Mahboob is the vice-chair of British Muslims for Secular Democracy, a charity which promotes religious understanding and addresses prejudice against Muslims. He says:

'Discrimination of any form is considered unacceptable in all civilised societies.

'The burqa or the niqab does just that. It allows one person to remain anonymous during face-to-face communication, thus depriving the right of the other to reciprocate whilst registering the changes in facial expressions, which is vital in such communication, in conjunction with voice that is used for everyday communication.

'Whether in public offices, educational institutions or out on the streets, the disadvantage to those who are required to deal with women covered under a niqab or burqa is immense.

AL JAZEERA

'Furthermore, to all the men out there, it is insulting since it implies that every man on the street would somehow get aroused by the sight of a woman's face and therefore to protect these women, they must be put behind a suffocating layer of thick clothing.

'The burqa or the niqab... allows one person to remain anonymous during face-to-face communication, thus depriving the right of the other to reciprocate whilst registering the changes in facial expressions'

'This might be true for certain societies where men rarely get a glimpse of women's faces or skin altogether, and any such sight might awaken their natural instincts.

'Whereas in Western societies, especially within the French society, this rationale does not hold much weight since members of the public are exposed to significant display of the skin of the opposite sex, which perhaps renders them immune to any such mental state where they would readily pounce on a woman upon seeing her uncovered face.

'The argument put forward by individuals and groups that somehow covering of women's faces is a religious obligation for the reason of their safety from the lewdness of men, falls flat on its face when recalling the etiquettes during Hajj.

'It should be remembered that during this holiest of pilgrimages, worldly pleasures and distractions have been removed by the Almighty, thereby allowing the pilgrims to concentrate on their prayers and associated rituals.

'During the Hajj, Islam forbids women from covering their faces, whilst at the same time removing segregation on the basis of sex during the days that men and women, who are otherwise strangers to each other, spend many days in close proximity to each other.

'No wonder even amongst the vast majority of women who do choose to cover themselves, only a fringe element finds the niqab or burqa a religious obligation, while the rest are content only with a hijab.

'Whether it's security at airports, identification in banks or during job or dole (income support) interviews, it is the right of the authorities and businesses to be certain of who they are dealing with on the basis of identity and communication.

'Furthermore, it is perfectly reasonable that the general public feel reasonably secure about the persons sharing the same public sphere. Not knowing whether an individual amongst them is a man or a woman due to their attire is deeply unsettling and any such anxieties must be addressed by the relevant changes to law.

'Burqa or niqab: neither has a place in Islam nor should it obtain a place in civilised Western societies where women are equal to men and public safety of all is paramount.'

28 January 2010

⇨ The above information is reprinted with kind permission from Al Jazeera. Visit http://english. aljazeera.net for more information.

© Al Jazeera

Two-thirds of Brits want burqa ban

Information from YouGov.

By Hannah Thompson

Two-thirds of the British public agree with the statement 'the burqa should be banned in Britain', our poll has found, in the wake of the ban on the niqab, or any face covering (with a few exceptions), coming into force in France this week.

We polled over 2,000 nationally representative British adults, in a question that explained the burqa is a loose garment worn by some Islamic women, which covers the face and body in public, and which is removed when the woman returns home to her household out of the view of men who are not her immediate family members.

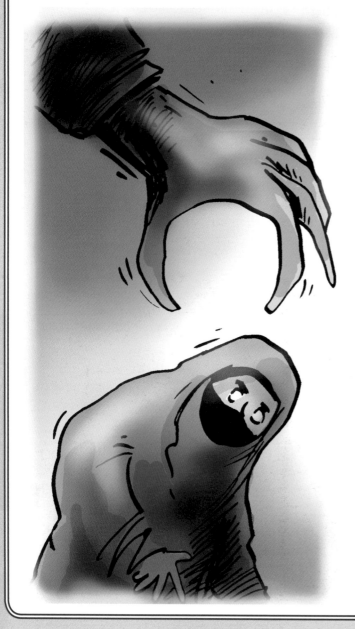

⇨ 66% agreed with the statement 'the burqa should be banned in Britain'.

⇨ 42% strongly agreed.

⇨ 27% disagreed with the statement, with 9% strongly disagreeing.

⇨ Men and women are largely in agreement over the issue (68% of men and 65% of women think it should be banned).

⇨ Older people are more likely than their younger counterparts to favour a ban (79% of the over-60s agreed with a ban, compared to 51% of those aged 18 to 24).

Freedom and human rights

The banning in France of anything which covers the face, notably and most controversially including some Islamic items of clothing like the burqa and niqab, has been the subject of fierce discussion and debate in recent months, with some saying it is right to end what they see as a coercive practice that inhibits women's freedom, and others arguing that dictating what people can and cannot wear infringes basic human rights.

According to the new law, any woman wearing a banned face covering, such as a burqa, can be fined up to €150 (around £130) and be made to take a citizenship class, and anyone found coercing a woman into covering her face risks severe penalties. Anyone who wishes to enforce the ban can legitimately ask a woman wearing such items to remove them, and can take her to the local police station or magistrate if she refuses.

Improving gender equality?

President Nicolas Sarkozy has championed the ban, prompting newspapers and blogs to comment on whether France is having an 'identity crisis'. For his part, Prime Minister François Fillon has attempted to neutralise the debate, referring to the bill as against 'covering one's face in public places', and emphasising that it aims to improve gender equality, not unfairly target Muslims.

Only a relatively small number of French Muslim women wear full-face coverings, it has been reported, from a Muslim population in France of five million. In contrast, Britain's Muslim population is around 2.4 million.

14 April 2011

⇨ The above information is reprinted with kind permission from YouGov. Visit www.yougov.com for more information.

YOUGOV

KEY FACTS

⇨ Buddhism began in Northern India over 2,500 years ago, and is based upon the teachings of Siddattha Gotoma who became known as the 'Buddha' – the enlightened one. (page 1)

⇨ Judaism is the faith of the Jews dating back over 4,000 years, originating in the Middle East. The Jewish community in Britain dates back to the Middle Ages. (page 3)

⇨ There are about a half-million Sikhs living in the UK. (page 3)

⇨ In a poll conducted by YouGov in March 2011 on behalf of the BHA, when asked the census question 'What is your religion?', 61% of people in England and Wales ticked a religious box (53.48% Christian and 7.22% other) while 39% ticked 'No religion'. (page 5)

⇨ By 2015, the level of church attendance in the UK is predicted to fall to 3,081,500 people, or 5% of the population. (page 6)

⇨ In a survey of 18,192 citizens of 23 nations worldwide, half (48%) agreed that 'religion provides the common values and ethical foundations that diverse societies need to thrive in the 21st century'. (page 7)

⇨ Just over half of people in Britain (52%) fear that the UK is deeply divided along religious lines and are particularly concerned about Islam compared with other faiths. (page 8)

⇨ Media coverage of popular religion, Christianity and public life, Islam and other religions and atheism and secularism has all gone up since the early 1980s. (page 13)

⇨ There has been an established Church in England since at least 1534. (page 14)

⇨ George Holyoake was the last man to be jailed in England for refusing to believe in God, in 1842. (page 15)

⇨ A study led by academics at Oxford University has concluded that believing in gods and an afterlife is part of human nature. (page 16)

⇨ A study found that people living in cities in developed countries were less likely to have religious beliefs than those living in rural areas. (page 16)

⇨ The present status of faith schools stems from the 1944 Education Act, which settled a long-standing dispute between Church and state over control of schools. In return for a degree of autonomy, church authorities were required to contribute financially to their schools. (page 17)

⇨ When surveyed, 88 per cent of local authorities believed that faith schools in their area were compliant with school admissions laws, when in reality just 47 per cent were, according to the Office of the Schools Adjudicator (OSA). (page 20)

⇨ A ComRes survey revealed that the majority of the British public believe that 'Equalities legislation has gone too far', with 61% thinking that 'Britain has become a country where the right to exercise freedom of conscience is being trumped by equalities law'. (page 25)

⇨ People are twice as likely to say the media is to blame for Islamophobia (29%) than far-right groups (13%), or indeed Muslims themselves either abroad (14%) or in the UK (11%). (page 33)

⇨ 23% of all serious acts of violence and vandalism perpetrated against Jews and Jewish property globally in 2010 took place in the UK, according to *Antisemitism Worldwide, 2010: General Analysi*s. (page 36)

⇨ Two-thirds of the British public agree with the statement 'the burqa should be banned in Britain'. (page 39)

⇨ Older people are more likely than their younger counterparts to favour a burqa ban (79% of the over-60s agreed with a ban, compared to 51% of those aged 18 to 24). (page 39)

Agnosticism

An agnostic believes that it is impossible to know or prove whether there is a god. The term 'agnostic' is also used for those who are sceptical of the existence of a god, but do not firmly commit to atheism.

Atheism

Atheism refers to the firm belief that there is no god or divine power at work in the universe, and human beings are constrained to one life only, with no continued existence after death.

Buddhism

Buddhism began in Northern India over 2,500 years ago. It is based upon the teachings of the Buddha, who sought to free himself and others from suffering and discover enlightenment.

Burqa

A burqa is a garment originally introduced by the Taliban in Afghanistan. It completely covers a woman's body and face, providing only a grille through which to see. It is distinct from the more common niqab, which leaves a slit for the eyes. The hijab is by far the most common garment worn by Muslim women in the UK, however: a headscarf which does not cover the face.

Christianity

Christianity is the largest religion in the world. Christians follow the teachings of Jesus Christ, who they believe to be the son of God, as given in the Bible – however, there are many different denominations and sects, with varying beliefs and rituals. These include Catholicism, Orthodox Christianity and Protestantism (which incorporates other groups such as the Methodists, the Baptists and the Church of England).

Faith school

A faith school is subject to the national curriculum, but is affiliated to a particular religious faith or denomination and reflects that in its teaching method and general outlook. Most faith schools are of a Christian nature.

Free school

Free schools have the same freedoms and flexibilities as academies, but they do not normally replace an existing school. Free schools may be set up by a wide range of proposers – including charities, religious organisations, businesses, educational groups, teachers and groups of parents.

Hinduism

Hinduism is an ancient Indian religion with no precise traceable beginning or single founder. Its central belief is in the existence of a natural order, a balanced way of living: physically, socially, ethically and spiritually.

Humanism

Humanism is a non-religious philosophy whose adherents propound an approach to life based on liberal human values and reason. Humanists believe that we do not need religious guidance in order to make moral choices. They believe that as this life is the only life we have, it is important to live it in an ethical and fulfilling way.

Islam

Islam is the second largest faith group in the UK today – 2.8% of the UK population were Muslims in 2001, according to the last census. Muslims believe in the word of Allah (God) as set out in their holy book, the Qur'an, by the prophet Muhammed in Arabia 1,300 years ago. Islam is a way of life, and followers must observe strict rules regarding diet, lifestyle and worship.

Judaism

Judaism dates back over 4,000 years, originating in the Middle East. The Jewish faith believes in one God who has revealed His will for them through their holy book, the Torah.

Religion

The word religion comes from the Latin *religio*, which means 'duty'. It can be defined as a set of beliefs, rituals and values centred around faith in a supernatural power at work in the universe. Major world religions followed in the UK today include Christianity, Islam, Hinduism, Sikhism, Judaism and Buddhism.

Sikhism

The Sikh tradition began in the Punjab region over 500 years ago. It was founded by Guru Nanak, the first teacher of the faith. Sikhs believe in one God, before whom everyone is equal. A good life is lived as part of a community, by living honestly and caring for others.

admission policies, faith schools 17–18, 20
anti-Muslim hate crime 28–30
anti-Semitism 36

bishops in House of Lords 6
Britain
  attitudes to religion 8
  as Christian nation 14
  and Islam 9–12
  religious beliefs 5–6, 15–16
Buddhism 1
burqa wearing
  arguments for and against 37–8
  prohibition in European countries 34–6
  public opinions 39

census data on religious belief 5
Christian evangelical free school 22
Christianity 1–2
  and Britain 14
  as default religion in Britain 15–16
  and equality legislation 25
  and the law 26–7
church attendance 6
citizenship and Muslims 9–10
constitution, British, and Christianity 14
creationism teaching at free school 22
curriculum and faith schools 19

democracy and Islam 10
discrimination
  against Christians 25
  against Muslims 30, 31–2
  at work 23–4

employment rights and religious belief 23–4
equality
  and faith schools 18–19, 20
  legislation, public opinion 25
Etz Chaim school 21–2
Everyday Champions Academy 22

faith schools 17–20
  and free schools programme 21–2
forced marriage and Islam 12
France and ban on burqa wearing 39
free school policy and faith schools 21–2
funding, faith schools 17

gender equality and Islam 12
government
  funding of faith schools 17
  and religion, public opinions 6

hate crime, anti-Muslim 28–30
Hindu schools 21
Hinduism 2

Holyoake, George 15
House of Lords and bishops 6
human nature and religious belief 16
humanism 4

integration into society 9
Islam 2–3
  in the UK 9–12
  see also Muslims
Islamophobia 30, 31–2
  and the media 33

Jewish free school 21–2
Jews, prejudice against 36
Jihad 11
Johns, Owen and Eunice 14, 25, 26
Judaism 3

Krishna Avanti primary school 21

law and religion 26–7

marriage and Islam 12
media
  coverage of religion 13
  and Islamophobia 33
mosques as hate crime targets 29
Muslims
  anti-Muslim hate crime 28–30
  British 9–12
  discrimination against 30, 31–2
  public attitudes to 33
  veiling of Muslim women 34–8
  see also Islam

niqab 37–8

parental choice and faith schools 19
philosophical beliefs 24
polygamy and Islam 12
public opinions
  on burqa wearing 39
  on impact of religion 7–9
  on religious involvement in government 6

recruitment equality, faith schools 18–19
religion
  and the law 26–7
  media coverage 13
religious belief
  in Britain 5–6, 8, 14, 15–16
  and discrimination 23–5
  as natural human inclination 16
  as negative and positive effects 7–8
  of staff, faith schools 18–19
  statistics 5–6
  in USA 6

religious discrimination at work 23–4

schools, faith 17–22
secularism
   as argument for banning burqa 36
   in Britain 15
security as reason for banning burqa 35
Sharia law 11–12
Sikhism 3
staff recruitment, faith schools 18–19
statistics on religious belief 5–6, 15–16
street violence, Muslim victims 29
suicide bombing, condemned by Muslims 10–11
surveys of religious belief 5–6, 8, 15–16

terrorism
   and Islam 10
   against Muslims 28

USA, religious belief 6

veils, Muslim women 34–9
violence against Muslims 28–30
violent extremism and Islam 10

Warsi, Baroness Sayeeda 31–2
women
   and Islamic face-veils 34–9
   Muslim, and hate crime 29
women's rights and burqa wearing 35–6
workers' rights and religious belief 23–4

ACKNOWLEDGEMENTS

The publisher is grateful for permission to reproduce the following material.

While every care has been taken to trace and acknowledge copyright, the publisher tenders its apology for any accidental infringement or where copyright has proved untraceable. The publisher would be pleased to come to a suitable arrangement in any such case with the rightful owner.

Chapter One: Religion in the UK

Faith and culture in the community, © Crown copyright is reproduced with the permission of Her Majesty's Stationery Office, What is humanism?, © British Humanist Association 2011, Religion and belief, © British Humanist Association 2011, Is religion a force for good in the world?, © Ipsos Global @dvisory, Religion today, © NatCen, Islam in the UK, © Islamic Society of Britain, Traditional practice may be down, but media coverage is up, © Religion & Society, What is 'Christian Britain'?, © Theos, Not atheist, not religious: typical Briton is a 'fuzzy believer', © Guardian News and Media Limited 2011, Oxford study: belief in God is natural, © Christian Today, Faith schools, © ATL, Faith school admissions may promote social inequality, © Runnymede Trust, Does God belong in the classroom?, © The Independent.

Chapter Two: Religious Tolerance

Religion or belief: rights at work, © ACAS, Has equalities legislation gone too far?, © ComRes, The law of England is not Christian, © Guardian News and Media Limited 2011, Islamophobia and anti-Muslim hate crime, © European Muslim Research Centre and University of Exeter 2011, Hatred of Muslims is one of the last bastions of British bigotry, © Telegraph Media Group Limited 2011, British public most likely to blame the media for Islamophobia, © ComRes, Fear factor: Europe bans the burqa, © openDemocracy, Anti-Semitism worldwide, 2010, © University of Manchester, For and against the face veil, © Al Jazeera, Two-thirds of Brits want burqa ban, © YouGov.

Illustrations

Pages 1, 16, 27, 34: Don Hatcher; pages 10, 24, 32, 39: Simon Kneebone; pages 8, 21, 29, 38: Angelo Madrid; pages 13, 31: Bev Aisbett.

Cover photography

Left: © James Knight. Centre: © Mira Pavlakovic. Right: © Yan Boechat.

Additional acknowledgements

With thanks to the Independence team: Mary Chapman, Sandra Dennis and Jan Sunderland.

Lisa Firth
Cambridge
September, 2011

The following tasks aim to help you think through the issues surrounding religion in society and provide a better understanding of the topic.

1 Read *Traditional practice may be down, but media coverage of religion is up* on page 13. Why do you think media coverage is rising when the number of people who define themselves as belonging to a faith and attend regular acts of worship has been falling? Discuss your views with a partner.

2 Choose one of the following faiths and find out more about its origins, what its members believe and how they worship: Christianity/Islam/Hinduism/Sikhism/Judaism/Buddhism/another faith of your choice (if you belong to one of these faiths, choose one other than your own to research). Write a summary of your findings.

3 Provide a glossary of Islamic words commonly used (often incorrectly) in the media, which would be informative to someone who knows little about the faith generally. Make sure you include the following words in your glossary: Sharia, Jihad, Fatwa, Burqa, along with any others you think would be useful. Read *Islam in the UK* on pages 9-12 as a starting point and follow up with your own research.

4 Visit the British Humanist Association website – www. humanism.org.uk – and find out more about this non-religious life philosophy. What do humanists believe? By what principles do they live their lives? What areas does the BHA currently campaign in? Prepare a short presentation about humanism and deliver it to your class.

5 Read *Is religion a force for good in the world?* on pages 7-8. Recreate the debate between Tony Blair and Christopher Hitchens as a class, debating the motion: 'Be it resolved, religion is a force for good in the world'. Half of you should argue for the motion and half against. One person should make notes on the points raised. When your debate is over, use a site such as YouTube to watch clips of the original Blair/Hitchens debate and see if any of the points they make correspond with yours.

6 Debate the following motion as a class, with one half arguing in favour and the other against: 'This house believes banning the burqa would be an unacceptable infringement of civil liberties: people have the right to choose what they can and cannot wear for themselves.'

7 Do you think Britain is still a Christian country? Do you think it ought to be? Are Christians unfairly discriminated against or marginalised in the UK today? Discuss your views in groups of three or four.

8 Why do you think so many British people – over 70% – describe themselves as Christian even though only a small proportion attend church regularly? Do you think taking part in organised worship is an essential part of belonging to a religion? What do you think is essential?

9 Read 'The Book of Dave', Will Self's novel which can be interpreted as a satirical comment on the origins of major world faiths. What points do you think it is trying to make? Do you support Self's view? Write a review.

10 'It is wrong to indoctrinate children into certain religions in so-called "faith schools". Education should be based on secular principle, so young people are able to make up their own minds about what they believe when they feel ready to do so.' Do you support or oppose this view? Write an essay analysing the role of faith schools: the benefits they can bring to communities and common criticisms of them, ending with your own conclusion as to whether you would support this statement.

11 Conduct a survey within your year group, asking everyone to answer the census question 'What religion are you?' by selecting from a list: Christian, Muslim, Sikh, Jewish, Hindu, Other, No religion. Then ask respondents to answer yes or no to the question 'Are you religious?' Present your findings in a series of graphs. Is the figure for those who say they have a religion the same as the figure for those who say they are religious? What conclusions can you draw?

12 Read a number of newspapers over a two-week period, including at least one broadsheet such as 'The Guardian' or the 'Daily Telegraph', and at least one tabloid such as the 'Daily Mirror' or 'The Sun'. Cut out any articles which refer to faith groups in the UK. At the end of this time, review the articles you have collected. Is the coverage mainly positive or mainly negative? Does one faith receive more coverage than others? Do you think media coverage of faith groups is proportionate?

13 Choose an influential person of faith, such as Mother Teresa or the Reverend Martin Luther King, and find out about their life and work. Write about how their religion influenced their life philosophy.